I0065185

AM I A COACH

SHORT STORIES OF INTENTIONAL ACTIONS

MARLEEN GEYEN

Copyright © 2024 Marleen Geyen
All rights reserved. ISBN: 979-8-89324-478-6
Printed in the United States of America.

No part of this publication shall be reproduced, transmitted, or sold in whole or in part in any form without the prior written consent of the author, except as provided by the United States of America copyright law. Any unauthorized usage of the text without express written permission of the publisher is a violation of the author's copyright and is illegal and punishable by law. All trademarks and registered trademarks appearing in this guide are the property of their respective owners. The opinions expressed by the Author are not necessarily those held by the Publishers.

The information contained within this book is strictly for informational purposes. The material may include information, products, or services by third parties. As such, the Author and Publisher do not assume responsibility or liability for any third-party material or opinions. The publisher is not responsible for websites (or their content) that are not owned by the publisher. Readers are advised to do their own due diligence when it comes to making decisions.

Table Of Contents

ACKNOWLEDGEMENTS

My heartfelt gratitude to the many amazing, generous, encouraging and supportive people who have worked alongside in my business adventures. Especially every staff person at Geyen Group South.

And to these individuals I want to thank you

Felicity Heffernan, Sheri Taber, JoLynn Marquass, Terri-lynn Mitchell, Dr. Lisa Schuenemann Brown, Z Hysell, Susan Jacobs, Cathy Sterner, Annie Geyen, Janie Geyen, Jim King, Rick Alvarez, Kristin Chiodi, Galina Kamenir, Sue Holmes, Jean Helgeson, Tim Roulette, for your commitment to friendship. And to Dolores Broll, Jean Keating, Jewel McKeon, Debby Crowder terribly missed but not forgotten.

Thanks to my husband, Fred, never backing away when our conversation began with "I have an idea"

Our children and their families, possibly the greatest teachers of living life boldly!

No one is an island, we are all connected.

Frank and Yanet,
Thank you for introducing me to all things Cuban.

BUSINESS WRITING REVEALS WHO I AM

When asked why I write the way I do and "expose myself" with my honesty, I respond with "it is the way that presents life in an open honest form".

It can be business writing, personal writing, or writing a friend's story, I find writing continues to make me show up and reveal who I am and it can be Frankenstein scary at times.

My writing style evolved from reading tons and tons of printed words about the what-why-how to manage a business. Small business ownership is front and center in my life, it is boldly important, and as I read all those "professional sounding theories" printed in the latest and greatest white papers I would throw up my arms and wonder how anyone as small-farm-girl as me could possibly follow all the steps and rules. I began my own story-telling truths about the knowledge and experiences I had and continue to have in owning a small business in Florida.

Then my professional writing, got somewhat crazier when I added personal experiences, and now I continue to talk from the page about feelings, understandings, and happenings. I even make up words once in a while.

In my world of women-owned businesses writing about personal stuff and straying away from the professional talk can be daunting because you see we are supposed to have it all together and act like professionals 24/7. In shorthand that means stiff upper lip and poise and proper and skirts.

I decided to squash all that and add to the definition of professional in ways that I hadn't seen or read before in the business mags. Because I believe there are some, a few, maybe one person who might benefit from reading about one woman's true thoughts and experience living the role of business owner while being a woman too.

Today I write business stories from what I see and hear in the office, learn from books and classes and understand from the speakers I meet at events. I love to add the humanness of looks, smiles, table-side talk, and eyes that dance with laughter when meeting a fun person in my writing.

And I write personal stories that talk about family, friends, and events.

Then I mix it together and if I am lucky, the business becomes the personal and the personal becomes the business. When that happens, I shout for joy, because honestly, in lives lived well I believe personal-business-professional all mix together like hamburger hotdish on a fall day in Minnesota.

Writing truly reveals who I am.

A GIANT AMONG US

When a friend of my niece died from a dangerous infection that took control of his body, I drove the distance to pay my condolences. At a small-town church, the life celebration was held on a Sunday afternoon, not all that far from my home. A beautiful drive on a fall afternoon.

This wasn't a business obligation, but a personal choice to show up in loving support.

The church was full to overflowing. Most were strangers, except for a few family members. I greeted my niece and family, and then, while walking out, I grabbed a 4" x 6" folded paper with his image on the front. I read the short descriptive paragraph changed my mind, and stayed for the service to hear what others had to say about this guy and the life he had lived for 61 years. So young, wasn't he?

Since I was not a church member, I sat near the back and took an aisle chair. Thus, I had an excellent site-line to the speaker and could hear the comments of others near me. I am fortunate I did.

A few brave people stood up, and a couple of others spoke from the podium. Now, remember the place was packed. Standing room only. Everyone, I mean every person I saw as I looked around, was entirely focused on the speaker every time a person spoke, and it didn't matter if it was the pastor, a brother, or someone who popped up and proceeded to tell their friend-story.

Do you understand? Every person that I could see from my aisle seat listened with eyes-forward to the speakers. No texting or phones ringing, which means the room was quiet and respectful.

I like to imagine this as "listening with our whole bodies."

Oh, what stories people told. From fishing, hunting, ballet, and opera to mentoring friendship and on-call support. He lived his life mainly within the confines of a small community.

Can you see it? A big bunch of people, quiet as mice, leaning earnestly forward to catch every word said.

Why?

As men and women raised to the moment and talked about this guy, they repeatedly spoke about the love they felt when near him, not in love words but in "this is what he did for me at the time." He loved others without question and was strong enough to show it every day in his way.

How do I know this? Remember, he was an unknown to me before the service. I was there because of my niece and her family.

I find this proof positive: so many were willing to speak about their first-hand interactions, and after all was said and done, the words were all in one accord, even though (this is the crazy part) the speakers were unrelated.

I want to end with this.

One guy shows love and humility and is willing to be transparent with his life choices, good and bad, and shows up every day.

A Giant Among Us. Life doesn't get better than that!

And I was so pleased I stayed for the service.

A WEDDING IN TENNESSEE

A good number of the family live in Tennessee. They moved from the "north" and made their homes in rural Tennessee amongst big trees, open fields, streams, a variety of shades of green, and gorgeous hills. The roads are windy, and trucks and cars drive slowly, and everyone waves at everyone.

Last summer, my great-niece sent me a wedding invite; the wedding was planned for the fall at a small country church, with the reception being held after in a nearby barn.

I was thrilled with the invite and even more thrilled that I could attend.

Flights were arranged, a VRBO was reserved, and a large pick-up was rented. I mean, really, when in Vegas or maybe Tennessee......The pick-up had huge tires, dark gray paint, and an extended bed a perfect status vehicle to be sure I fit right in.

Because I had never been where I was going, I would be lying if I said I didn't have a few worries. The first of which was would espresso coffee be available anywhere near. Will I understand the other wedding guests' southern talk, and if I get lost in the hills, will the navigation still transmit on the truck?

Basically, though, my main concern was will I represent my family in the way and light my great-niece would be proud of.

I found myself out of my professional comfort zone.

With these thoughts, I arrived at the church, found a parking spot next to a line of other trucks, walked through the front doors with a touch of nervousness, and found my seat. Nieces and nephews, I hadn't seen in months came up to hug and say hi. The sanctuary was beautifully arranged with comfortable seating and filled with a person in every seat. Truly, it was the people that drew me in, except for family. All the other wedding guests were complete strangers, and yet they treated me like I was a friend. Nodding heads and open faces welcomed me.

Immediately after the service, we moved the wedding celebration to the barn next door. The barn wasn't polished or spit-shined or painted white, but warm and happy and inviting and lovely and decorated for a wedding party. Guests were milling around everywhere, and after dinner was served, the music began. This family is musically talented so obviously so that the family musicians lined up to pay tribute and perform for their beautiful niece in celebration of her wedding day. Dancing came next with young and old breaking a leg on the floor.

How refreshing to be in this barn dancing to the beat and feeling the love and acceptance and joy of so many people; it felt like a collective joy.

The night got old, and the party ended. I returned home, and a few months later, I received a thank you card from my great-niece. The card was a printed message with an added thoughtful and kind handwritten note on the back.

Her note laid to rest my concern about representing the family in a way that would make her proud. I am grateful.

ASKING QUESTIONS AND GIVING LOVE

My son asked me why I show up the way I do with grandkids. He was wondering why I say this and that and never admonish or argue, even when he knows I do not agree or think like these young adults and younger yet, kids.

What an effortless response this was for me. My job is to give nothing but love.

My job, role, and responsibility as a grandmother are to love my grandkids. Sure, when asked, I share opinions and experiences and funny things, but never a criticism passes my lips.

Not my job. My job is to live and act congruently with the person I am.

Recently, I witnessed a parallel with this same principle.

An accident involving Yorkis rear-ended and side-ended by another vehicle. No fault of his except to be on the road.

Many questions were asked, and all were answered with total clarity by Yorkis. His actions were supported by the vehicle's camera film.

Another driver in a white car did not pay attention and caused the collision. When an insurance adjuster admonished my driver, I was not happy. Because the truth was that the insurance company's problem with Yorkis is that he is 18 years old. Too young, they believe in driving a company vehicle.

Do I agree with the insurance adjuster and confuse my driver? I did not criticize yell, or correct. What I did was talk to Yorkis one-on-one and tell the story from the viewpoint of the insurance adjuster. I lead the conversation confidently, believing in who we are as a company and how often others may get it wrong.

And then, I sat back to evaluate our interaction. Questions, responses, Yorkis and myself, back and forth, asking and responding with respect and listening. And yes, asking questions and giving love telegraphs outside the family.

In a nutshell, asking questions and giving love shows up through voice, words, eyes, expressions, energy, and body language every time we speak. This makes me happy!

Think about it.

BOOTS TO A RESCUE

When expectations are high, and confidence is a top priority, I always wear boots to the business meeting. Everywhere, anywhere the meeting is held, boots work for me in that they add "act as if" so I keep a pair close because you never know when needed.

This is what happened at one of our accounts and led to an urgent meeting.

A few of my technicians working with me were doing their job of cleaning carpet in a facility when a film-taker appeared and began to film the work they were doing. I got the call a few minutes later, asking what was going on. Neither the film-taker nor his assistant had any answers just that the film person was doing his job and had been directed to take a video of the work we were doing that evening.

As you can imagine my technicians did not appreciate the feeling of being "watched and critiqued" while doing the job which they are certified and trained to do. Not only watched and critiqued, but the filming felt like a violation of privacy in the cleaning systems we use in our business.

I was angry right along with my staff. They finished the job, returned to the shop and I promised to get answers.

Early the next morning I contacted by phone call and email the person in charge of this account. I included his boss in the email and asked for a meeting ASAP. A three-way meeting was arranged for the day after. Me, contact and contact's boss in the main conference room of the company.

Here is where my boots came in.

The night before the meeting, I took a serious look at the pairs of boots I had lined up and ready to do battle. I chose a black pair with 2-inch heels, knowing the contact was about 5'10". Making me closer to his height and adding a sense of equality in physical stature.

Let me backtrack a little here: boots do not speak to me in words. I am not crazy and hearing things, but they do add a feeling of all-is-right-in-the-world. Thus, I often can be seen in a pair no matter the weather or temperature and most certainly when a power meeting is scheduled.

I arrived right on time for the morning meeting. The contact met me at the elevator doors, and we walked to the conference room. We entered, and I sat down in the leather chair at the head of the large oak table leaving both contact and his boss chairs on either side. They chose to sit across from one another down a few spaces from me, and the meeting began.

When I left 15-20 minutes later, I had an agreement that this would not happen again, and I had an understanding that even though filmmaking was new to myself and the staff, it was not all that unusual with this company.

Back to the boots. Whatever adds spark, confidence, assurance, "act as if" for you Might be a specific shirt or hat, jean color or suit or socks or quote or rabbit foot? Whatever works.

BUSINESS OWNERS DO WHAT EXACTLY?

Runners run, writers write, teachers teach, and what do serious business owners do?

They do business. They interpret and add meaning to a column of long numbers.

A powerful business, as I see it from my personal experience, is all about fulfilled employees and satisfied customers. Business is considered trade, employment, work, profession, and occupation; another way to say this is money in and money out.

When I attended business classes and training, I didn't understand the employee part. I understood the money in was revenue and the money out was expenses and viewed the many numbers in neatly organized rows on white paper as numbers, unrelated to real people.

It wasn't until I was the owner of a business and the money in and the money out that I understood that every number represents, in one way or another, a life, a person, a human being.

Example: Income/customer account pays $$$ for the cleaning service offered. A person must coordinate on the customer side the desired service; simply put, the coordinator now has a job with a job description. The service contractor is paid/income to perform the service.

Example: Expense/ payroll is a no-brainer but how about the telephone, internet, insurance, auto repair? All expenses to a business, but if we dig somewhat deeper the expense is also income to the utility or repair company.

This can be expanded to every dollar moved back and forth in every business.

Money in, money out.

What I saw was that what is income for one company is an expense for another, but the truth of the matter is, at the end of the day, all the $$$ inter-changed in some manner is abundantly more than just income and expense but rather affects real live people. Employees are paid no matter their title or job position, and every business has one or more employees. Income money in for one company is Expense money out for another.

One could bravely say that every dollar in a transaction translates to human change.

The numbers are only and simply symbols of something far greater.

When I began to put faces behind each and every number in my reports, my decisions changed, and my business took on a living, breathing presence for me.

Strange as this may sound, I found out that the higher the numbers, not only were the number of people affected, but the business was affected exponentially.

Who knew? I did not learn this in a class, but with experience and by diving deep into the essence and energy of what makes a business function profitably and honorably.

When I got this, I mean really got this, I read my financials differently. No longer were the perfectly arranged columns, only numbers. The columns had human faces.

BUSINESS CLIFF NOTES

When asked about the best and most efficient way to keep a business up and running during this economic time, I had to stop and catch my thoughts before answering.

I own a commercial carpet cleaning business, and you know what? People are not in the office these days.

I dream about feet walking on office carpet, like the old days!

Red high-heeled shoes, black flats, brown oxfords, rubber soles, leather bottoms, and mud-tracking sports shoes.

There is this thing about footwear, they all track in dirt, germs, and soil that leaves spots, and for a commercial carpet cleaning business, we love the earth.

But for today, tomorrow, and next week, there will be fewer office people sitting in cubicles, offices, and conference rooms than there were three years ago.

Since we need the dirt to do our cleaning job, and no one is bringing it in and leaving it on the carpet, there is certainly less need for our service. Many of our accounts are on hold because of this lack of dirt.

I do not know how other companies are working this out, but here we are, asking our technicians to work with us. So, take a vacation, trade-off hours with each other, and be flexible.

Yes, it is about employees. I believe we can make it through this time if everyone is on board. Our cleaning accounts will be back in some fashion, maybe not the way we scheduled in the past, but asking us to do the service when necessary in the upcoming weeks.

I have always drilled down about wages, and still today, I worry about salaries, sit and doodle about wages, and plan the following month's wage schedule.

Now, this leads me to the beginning. When asked about the best, most efficient, and ideal way to keep the business going, I replied with "wage security for everyone." And the caveat to this is nothing has changed from my focus three years ago. Only today do the wage puzzle pieces move more frequently to fit.

BUY, STEAL, OR HOARD

Sitting at the boardroom table, our eldest technician listens and watches. Finally, he quietly speaks a few Spanish words to the newbie. I do not know what he says, but the newbie smiles and nods.

This is how I saw wisdom yesterday at the staff meeting with everyone in attendance.

Many people think about wisdom, what it is, what it does, and who has it. But I have not seen wisdom explained as a way of being. An inside job, you might say. Shows up unexpectedly, and if you are not paying attention, puff, and it is gone.

The eldest technician arrives early, smiles often, has the respect of the whole, and keeps this persona intact all the time. No change, no drama, and a pleasure to be around, even when no one is speaking.

When I first recognized this, I wondered if he was an outcast because of his age, so I watched group dynamics and discovered no, that was incorrect. Instead, I found him sharing his wisdom in a gentle way. A short conversation, body language, eye talk, and laughter, all from his source of knowledge deep within.

I ponder this regularly: what is the easiest way to get wisdom? And as I watch and listen and learn, I believe wisdom shows up in our way of being. Truly, wisdom cannot be stolen, bought, or hoarded.

Wisdom shows itself in my business through our eldest technician and his way of being.

We are fortunate.

BUYING A BUSINESS IN 2021
More than numbers

I have been an owner of a small boutique business and felt I had reached the saturation I wanted in the local market, and now I was sticking my toe in another service and looking for a way to employ more people. I began to look at another small business that would complement the current service we were already doing.

Then the virus hit, and revenue dropped, and I began swimming upstream along with my employees and the business we were in.

Before I had been looking, now I was buying. So, after 6 months of steadily reviewing financials, I decided on one that looked like a match. Made the offer, the buyer accepted, and I was off and running to get the details worked out and the closing date set.

A couple of months later, the date of closing was here, and I had all my ducks in a roll and ready to go immediately after the money was transferred to the seller.

-transfer of the website

-transfer of phone

-insurance requirements

-bank loan

-transfer of trailer title

Every duck in the roll fell through the cracks. Luckily, I was able to scrabble together the funds at the last minute to close on the scheduled date and the loan, which came through 3 weeks later. As for the rest of the list... back and forth dealing with people in charge to process accounts and update with new business owner information.

I am still waiting for accountability for the transfer of needed information and internet sites.

I felt violated, not heard, heart hurt, not in control, and had no answer to how to make people do the job they said they could do and deliver when they said they would deliver, and then I RELAXED.

Looking from a higher view, I saw myself sitting back and letting go of what I could not control and looking at what I could. First off, my attitude and the certainty that this was the right path forward and then my continued encouragement to the people I work with.

Now, a few more weeks have passed, and I have thought long and hard about this. The accounts are not shaping up as promised, but every staff member is on board and is stepping up to do what needs to be done.

Success is more than numbers. When we add human value, it becomes PRICE-LESS.

What more could I ask for?

CAN YOU FEEL IT

We were sitting out in the backyard on bright blue plastic lawn chairs last weekend, talking about valuable beginner instructions while driving a standard transmission car. Jerk, jerk, dead stop.

Gas, clutch, brake, gas, clutch, stop. If you have ever learned to motor a standard clutch/shift car, you get what I am saying.

But after a few or many stops and starts, it is miraculously true......you feel it. And away you go, driving effortlessly. We had a good laugh sharing our personal stories to make you feel it.

But honestly, you do, and soon driving with the clutch/brake/gas pedals becomes like riding a bike, no thought but an automatic movement of the clutch in, brake, and shift.

After leaving the family that afternoon, I began to think about the term, you feel it.

How many times I have heard guys say small business is not about warm and fuzzy feelings. It's numbers, research, and data. Yes, I agree, it is. But I found out it is also more. Sorry guys.

I ventured into owning a small business by first understanding the numbers. Every single dollar was accounted for and assigned to either an expense or income on the profit and loss report, and I made darn sure I could tell the difference and explain how the numbers came to be on the other reports as well.

So, there you go, numbers in, numbers out. I had it down pat and kept at it religiously every week. Then I noticed trends in the business, and then I noticed the exciting feeling that I got before I needed to make a change, and I questioned myself continuously because that perception or sense or feeling stuff was not written about in the black-and-white business materials I read.

Mostly, I realized I felt the business vibe, which is a momentum that runs throughout the business. Staffing and changing systems, asking the right questions, and partnering with the right vendors, right meaning right for my business, which may not be right for your business.

I like to say the feeling is the business vibe, it shows itself not only to the owner but also employees and it does not diminish the importance of facts, figures, and reports, but adds the importance of feeling/knowing where to go from here, like who is the best hire and the best partner.

This is a short blurb on how I came to believe in and trust feelings as a business owner, it surely is not complicated. I did find that understanding and acting on the feel/vibe of my business took time, not weeks, not months, but years to see all of it; the numbers and understanding and feeling the business, all in alignment to make the business successful.

If I were to teach, can you feel it in a small business class the outline would look something like this?

Why are you in business?

Who are you working with both staff and vendors and clients?

What is your experience in your business?

Let's talk about the numbers, reports, and book keeping

Finally, we will explore the feel of a good decision as it relates to your business.

And I would say from my experience, that just as motoring a standard transmission vehicle, once you feel it in your business, you are on the road to keeping it going and are ready and able to teach this to another.

CASE IN POINT

When writing and posting, I aim to write what is true. I keep tripping over truth because it can change.

Case in point.

Truth: the business of commercial carpet cleaning in Florida is considered a commodity service, that being so, the price point that employees earn per hour is minimum wage or below minimum wage.

Truth: I got my business experience working in Minnesota and there the commercial carpet cleaning industry is viewed in a different way. Employees are paid a good wage; in all the years I worked in Minnesota I never knew what the minimum wage was as it had no effect on the pay scale of the staff I hired.

Truth: But now I worked in Florida and had to come to grips with the wage disparity.

I leaned to black and white outcomes, views, and decisions for a zillion years until the truths that I held were no longer true. How odd is that?

This is where I stumbled though. I believe certified commercial carpet cleaning technicians are valuable and not easily found in employee pools of job hunters. To put my money where my mouth is I decided early on to pay above minimum wage, market wage or normal wage for this job designation.

I have kept to this decision for over 15 years and find now when minimum wage is supposed to be at $15.00/hour in a few years, doesn't change this business truth: certified commercial carpet cleaning technicians = good wages.

CHASING EMAILS

I worked on a refinance project and eagerly submitted all relevant documents within 24 hours. I kept checking my inbox for a responding email from my financial contact. A couple days went by, and I wondered what professional courtesy is before I contacted them once more.

I was under a lot of pressure and an unmovable deadline for the funds that the re-fi would deliver. Which lead to my impatience with this person. I mean, really, how long does it take to do this job?

Sound familiar? Waiting on an email. Thinking about this, I started to remember and go over the last month or so of waiting for email responses. I found out that many, about a third, of emails I sent, I either had to resend again or call or text the person to find out the information I asked for in my first email.

This was extremely frustrating and time-consuming in rechecking inbox and junk mail.

So, I reached for Google to ask, "what is the expected time for an email to be returned."

Guess.

Surveys conducted by Microsoft and Klaus found that 50% of email senders expect a reply within 24 hours, while a more recent one by HubSpot shows that 90% of customers expect an "immediate" response, that being 10 minutes or less. Jul 7, 2020

Short answer: as fast as you can.

Long answer: within 24 hours

A short "I received your email and will get back to you within----" is a reasonable expectation even if someone is extremely busy.

So, I decided to add this short line in my emails to business contacts and a few family members.

I want to be sure you got this email. It would be much appreciated if you could respond with a short "got it" and possibly let me know when you can react.

 Does this solve the email response time? It helps.

As for the refinance project, it was handled, and I got the money!

CONTACTING VENDORS 101

When have you tried to get a real person on the other end of the phone line while looking for good service, it's almost impossible! I recently made an account change and explored the online chat-way of communication. After a few chat messages, I typed "I WANT TO TALK TO A REAL PERSON" because you see I realized that the answers I was getting were preprinted posts that may include a word or two from my chat question in the preprinted post body but didn't begin to address the question I had. Obviously, this was not working for me.

Last month I contacted 2 vendors to straighten out the account I have with each, after 6 calls to one and 3 to the other I have yet to be sure the changes are accurate. Right now, I am feeling frustrated, unimportant, and downright angry.

HOW TO REMAIN CALM WHILE CONTACTING VENDORS 101

Not sure what a beginner class on contacting vendors would include but it might be a class worth creating and presenting in a classroom setting. But wait, the registration may well fill within seconds of the class offering. No kidding.

Okay, I didn't feel justified about this rant until I found out that I am not the only person facing this drama. My landlord had a similar experience and then he gave up. A friend rolled her eyes when I explained my dilemma, my brother, my kids, my sister and the list go on.

Last night I had yet another unresponsive interaction, the online chat was wasted minutes. After the useless chat, I had an insight into my own business and our staff and how we answer and respond to customers. I like personal touch during business hours, always a real person on the other end of a call. When it's not possible, returned calls within a short time.

I want connection when I call or reach out in some way, I want a response, and I don't think I am an anomaly. I want answers to my questions and honestly many times I want to be seen and heard, recognized, and respected.

At my office, this works best when we give out direct cell numbers of staff.

I am committed to working with customers in answering their questions in the way that works best for them. Is it a text? A phone call or email, no matter the form we will be sure that we are available. We are real live people here.

OUR PROMISE: tell us the best way to respond to you and we will do our best to be there for you.

Our staff is available during business hours to take your call. Once you are a customer you will have a direct line to the person who manages your service.

We may not be an international company and doubt that is in our future BUT we are a human company and we promise to connect in a human respectful manner.

This message began from not being heard by 2 vendors in the last few months, I see a change in the future, a change where being seen and heard is the most important value a business can give.

Now we need to come up with a way to do it!

CONTROL MATTERS

This has been a month of late deliveries, rescheduled cleanings, changes in staff, and leaving any control I thought I had at the door, outside, in the cold.

So, I ask myself, "why does control matter in the here and now?" And when I have it, I am a happy person; without it? Sad face.

The incident that made me think was a delivery scheduled for this week. This morning, I learned from the trucking company that it was not happening. Not this week or next week. First thought, go and get the machine, deliver it where it is scheduled, and end the story. Then reality showed up. The machine is 800 pounds, and I haven't the required trolley or lift at my disposal, much less the muscle to steer the machine into the planned space. So, uncontrollably, here I am, waiting a couple more weeks.

This latest no-control would only be concerning if the client was waiting for me to show up with the machine. So now, I pass on the specifics, and the problem expands.

What is the saying "expectation is the basis of unhappiness?"

That's the beef. Control seeps away when working with others, not being the person calling the shots. And what is left expectation? A new saying might be, "unclarified and misunderstood expectation is the basis of unhappiness."

Sometimes control is up to each individual and can be managed by driving a vehicle, eating and drinking, or having discussions with friends. This control of self is a lovely feeling of freedom and autonomy.

Not this week, though. The unexpected delivery delay was out of my control.

But then again, the delivery time needed to be clarified and stated.

Next time: clear understanding of time and day.

Because even within a group of more than one decision-maker, control does matter.

CRAP HAPPENS

Is it what we did? Was it given to us, or was it there already?

I love God, Spirit, Source, Earth, and everything that goes with it. But when I think of the whys, I stumble. Like when I felt a migraine coming on. Was it because I wasn't relaxed, clear, thankful, sending light, drinking enough water, eating the best food, or sleeping on the wrong pillow? Maybe it was payback for something I did or a warning about what was to come.

Who knows.

So let me bring this down to the common denominator of questions.

I want answers to basic questions.

Others want to explain why their beliefs answer my questions.

I found something so exciting to me during my search for honest answers.

I found that beliefs are remarkably alike. Lifting us from harm, healing, wanting the best, future hope.

But in all beliefs, crap continues to happen. No magic cure. We live the good and live through the pain by moving and breathing.

Simple honesty feels like the answer to my questions.

MARLEEN GEYEN

CAFFEINE SPEAKS A LANGUAGE

Is it a long black or short white? Espresso or latte? Grande or venti? Dark or light?

Coffee shop meetings are as comfortable as the coffee I order. When my feet step into a coffee shop, I feel the love. So, when I have a friend, business associate, or stranger sit with me at a small counter or table, I already am halfway happy with our meeting results. And I give all the credit to the coffee! I do.

I decided to see if I could prove this true, so I evaluated coffee shops, people I meet there, décor, smell, and location. Sure, I have a few local favorites, but by and large, I found the staff and customers at coffee shops are interested in coffee, that is a given, but also you will discover creatives who stop and sit and reflect and dream. Authors, business owners, mothers with infants, students, emergency workers, blue-collar, white-collar, no-collar people like coffee and the jolt of being in a place where acceptance is well, just that acceptance.

I travel some, and since I have this theory about shops in the US, I decided to try it out in international shops. Not so easy since I am not a regular out-of-country traveler, but nevertheless, I decided to have a go when I am out of the country. If only I could record these excursions as a business expense!

I have read that people believe beer is the pleasurable international drink of choice. Maybe I doubt that because I am not a beer drinker, I would argue the global drink of choice is coffee, or in parts of Asia, tea. Caffeine, nonetheless. I have found and drank rich, dark, flavorful coffee in the most out-of-the-way destinations; a small village shop in Tanzania, an Irish pub, a Polish bakery, a Cuban street corner, a New Zealand wharf coffee shop.

If I were an international business advisor or financial executive, I would hold all confidential meetings at the local famous coffee shop, anywhere in the world. Because it is there that there is instant familiarity within the warm coffee culture, understanding that just might add to the success of the meeting. But the real secret is that caffeine speaks a language of connection and agreement.

DEBBY'S TEXTS

Debby and I talked occasionally by phone and met for lunch every few months but what cemented our friendship were her texts. Her texts felt like a roaring fire in the fireplace, a warm quilt in the winter, a soft rainbow in the sky. She wrote as the corporate executive she was, direct and knowledgeable, caring and connected.

Then Debby got sick. Not a head cold, virus or broken toe, but something more sinister and uncontrollable. Lunches were now more intense and less regular. The booth where we met was reserved for us for an hour or maybe two. The vinyl was unforgiving and so often we left early when sitting became too uncomfortable for Debby to stay.

No longer able to see each other face to face regularly, we began to speak by text. Each text I got was like a love note. So clear and straight from the heart and funny too. Debby had a way with languages, I think she spoke 6, and she would correct me in my texts when another word was better suited for our text conversing. We laughed by text, we cried and we planned our future times together.

8 years and counting from the initial diagnosis Debby passed. Her texts remain. And in these precious texts is the image of her spirit, her sense of humor, her direct thoughts, her disagreements with life, her love. I doubt she knew that when she posted these thoughts of hers by text that she was leaving behind a fraction of her legacy.

RUSS: I was a student in a story-skill workshop recently and wrote this short story about Debby. I thought you might enjoy it and maybe even bring out a smile.

I remember and talk to Debby every day, usually it's just "oh Debby". I believe she would understand that. What a lovely beautiful human.

Thinking of you too, at times words fall short.

Please know that you are loved and, in our thoughts, and conversation often.

DECISION FATIGUE

On a business trip last month, I was a ride-along. Meaning I was not the person making the decisions of which road, which hotel, which diner, which car rental. Even though I was not the one in charge I was asked for my opinion. This ride-along position soon became painful. Many small decisions in three days when one and done echoed in my brain. Easy to say "how about making a decision and if there are no visible negatives, go with it." And let's not revisit the decision, period!

By the second day, I was exhausted and questioned myself as to why? These were small decisions, ongoing sure, but in the scope of the business being done, not serious.

Until I realized that I was making decisions back and forth about the same question or circumstance. Ugh. First this way, then that, then back to this, enough I said to myself. And I titled this back and forth as "Decision Fatigue". Because was I ever fatigued!

Dizzy from the back and forth surrounding the same questions and arriving at decisions that honestly didn't much matter one way or the other, I stopped the madness and made a pact within myself that I would give my opinion or preference once and disengage as to the outcome.

It worked! I immediately felt less stress and you might even say "peaceful" in my once-only decision on outcomes that were preference-based and ones that I could easily flow with whatever was decided.

I recognize that not everyone has the one-and-done brain feature and I make allowances for those people, as I did with my companion on the three-day trip. The three days were unapologetically the first time I got the whole Decision Fatigue thing. With this awareness, it will be much easier to spot it and act accordingly.

I might not be an ideal candidate for group cruises.

DISCOVERING THE UNEXPECTED

A couple of weeks ago, I had the opportunity to spend a few days in Lexington and Staunton, Virginia. A new experience. I have never been to the area, and I was determined to make the best use of my short time there.

So, I walked the old streets and visited old cemeteries and learned more about Confederate history than I ever knew. Like Stonewall Jackson's first name is Thomas, and he lived in Lexington on a sloping street with a kitchen garden in the back. I visited his home and found out details about him and his family and the history of the enslaved people who worked for him. It was incredible. The curator at Jackson's house was terrific. Especially for someone like me with a lot of questions. The place was pretty cool, and the dinner at the restaurant across the street was a satisfying way to end the day.

Do you know that Washington and Lee University and Virginia Military Institute are in Lexington? This was news to me as I walked both campuses, met students, and was reminded of the valuable lesson of an open mind.

I thought this short Virginia trip was about seeing the sights, overeating, and coming back with a pleasant experience.

It was more.

The cemetery in Staunton has a huge grassy hill right in the middle. I walked up to read the marker. Over 700 Confederate soldiers are buried there, with no name's plaques, only grass. I sat down to catch my breath and think about commitment.

This post is not about the South vs. North but humanness, loyalty, family, and history. Not right or wrong, but leaning in to understand our American history.

Because I was born in the North and had not opened myself up to history as such, I found my visit to both small towns, Lexington and Staunton, enlightening. I felt connected somehow, which sounds crazy,

We may wish to erase history in today's world, but we cannot without erasing the importance of freedom and humanity and how we arrived where we are today. So how do we understand events from our armchair discussions without venturing out into the world to see the actions that make up the truth?

I bought a book titled: Stonewall Jackson's Book of Maxims. It is a good read and valid today as it was in the 1860s. The cover has a sepia image of the man.

I am going back, maybe not to Staunton and Lexington, but to other places to soak in more of what makes us Americans.

DISCOVERING SOCKS THAT GIVE AND GIVE

Another year, what to buy, another year, what to buy. It is nearing Christmas and I was in a funk about what to buy that has meaning. Not another shirt, boot or hat, and they are good gifts but I was looking for something with more punch and more meaning.

All four kids, 2 girls and 2 boys, were in their teens or early 20's. so the stocking stuffers I bought in the past wasn't cutting it anymore. Little people toys, match-box cars, Legos or small dolls were not on their Christmas lists. What works, what makes sense and what would they appreciate I continued to ask myself. I was feeling overwhelmed and underappreciated in the gift giving arena, this was mind boggling and with my kids and their individual tastes I didn't want to mess it up.

I want to back up a moment to say that I hadn't been the best example of a caring mom when it came to giving to not-for-profit organizations. Sure, we gave to our place of Sunday church, but when it came to community charities, I scored a big fat F. This bothered me and now with the gift giving time of year approaching I wondered how I could introduce a more giving mindset at this point of my and their lives and impress on them that there are more ways to make a difference that are equally important and worthy when the focus is on causes, personal projects and international charities.

While browsing through the internet looking for just the right gifts, I found a site where you buy a pair of shoes and the company, TOMS, then gives a pair to someone in desperate need. This fit what I was looking for and so I bought everyone in the family the original black pair of TOMS shoes. And I passed on the story of TOMS during our Christmas Eve party, in between the shrimp, the cheese platter and the tapioca pudding eating.

OK now I was on a roll. The next year I found this sock company, BOMBAS, nice socks by the way, where I could buy a pair and they give a pair to someone affected by homelessness! This was more perfect than shoes because socks are the most wonderful stocking stuffers. And the kids loved these socks so much that last Christmas a few were showing off the socks they had gotten the past year and were now talking about colorful new socks they were hoping to get in their Christmas stockings this year.

Sock getting has become every year stocking stuffer gift now, it's expected, appreciated, welcome and fun! This year we were at 16 sock receiving grandchildren and adults, in sock language that is 16 pairs to get and 16 pairs to give.

DOES IT FEEL NATURAL

It was a match made in heaven when I was looking for a way to meet women who owned small businesses in Uganda and Tanzania, that I, fortunately, met someone who worked with these organizations and she graciously allowed me to tag along with her on one of her administrative trips.

I have always been intensely interested in women who work in their creative small business and at the same time are the sole provider for their families. This was working their business without the backup of medical insurance or the support of their country's government or local organizations or relatives or savings. These women have no one to "watch their back" in case Plan A fails.

For them, there is no Plan B and I learned that first-hand while in Uganda.

How grateful I was to be invited to a weekly gathering and see firsthand the women, their seriousness and commitment, their business acumen, friendly manner, and curious questions.

Before I get further into my story, please allow me to tell you about my first visual impression of Kampala, Uganda.

Our delayed flight arrived in the early morning hours and we taxied immediately to the hotel to grab a few hours of sleep before meeting our driver, Charles. Fast sleep and fast breakfast and we were on the sidewalk stepping into the small gray van Charles had ready for us, I was breathless in anticipation. As we began our morning on Kampala streets I saw people everywhere, walking, running, and riding in packed buses, small vehicles packed with passengers, bikes, and motorbikes, every vehicle filled to the brim and overflowing with passengers beginning their day, I was speechless. I couldn't talk. I couldn't think, only look. So much humanity, up close and personal.

The city was unlike any I had ever visited before. The people were unlike any I had met before. The poverty, other-worldliness of where I was at that exact moment, I had no voice to explain.

Three hours later I began to collect my thoughts and able to give them a voice. didn't though. I kept my thoughts to myself because the person I was with and our driver were familiar with Kampala, they weren't first-time visitors as I was.

In the twinkling of an eye, I was changed, I was aware of the pressing needs of humanity all around me. It was a serious, heavy, slap-in-the-face reality of the daily lives of a million people living in the city.

And then I met Betty at the gathering I was invited to join. Betty had a small business in what was considered the worst slum in Uganda. Betty's business was medicine in a backpack. Her days were filled with visits to the women in her neighborhood and there she distributed malaria-preventing tents, bandages, ointments and taught the basics of good hygiene amid poverty. That was Betty's business description, what she really did as I watched her teach a small class inside her home was offer hope and love. And Betty did that extremely well.

It felt natural to be there in the midst of women so like me!

There were other business women at this gathering, owning various displays of businesses, clothing, fruits, charcoal, meat. We are talking small here, one room or one stall at the market but so darn happy to be providing for their family.

So much similarity between me and them, I was honored to be accepted and asked questions and more than grateful to be able to ask my own questions and seeing their eyes light up with joy as they talked about what they do every day in their business, no weekend or holiday breaks.

When an event, trip or book, or person makes such an impact on your life, how can words that are written fully explain? I haven't figured that out yet.

The best I can write is that I didn't want to come home, I wanted to be there walking with them and sitting with each one at their businesses stand/cart/room and assist in the service they provide in their community.

LIGHT-BULB ON: this is the same way I feel here at home. Community, service, small business, women who own businesses.

My time in Uganda left a forever change. Poverty as I had never seen before stopped up my voice. And Betty, I will never forget her as she was a witness to all good that happens when someone loves and cares for a neighbor and a community.

Forever Grateful.

EMERGENCY ROOMS MAY BE UNDERRATED

Emergency rooms may be underrated.

When my Mom was there last week, we had an up-close and personal look. Mom's first-class seat was the bed and mine the wooden rocking chair.

Mom had a variety of questionable symptoms including shortness of breath, weakness, and cough. I had no symptoms and volunteered as the taxi driver and along for the ride.

Mom's voice was hoarse when we got to the hospital. Mom was admitted and immediately hooked up to an IV, one in each arm and a blood pressure cuff dangling from a forearm. I look longingly at the cuff thinking I would like one too, knowing full well that this was going to be a long day.

While we waited for test results, we were entertained by the orchestra of noise serenading us. First were the dings, then the beeps, after that the bong, and lastly the beep-beeps. Not counting footsteps in the hall, beds being rolled in the hallway, crying, voices, and telephones. I didn't have the words to add to this background music and neither did Mom. We kept up some kind of conversation in the midst of it all.

Emergency rooms are a world unto themselves. It's like a small universe beneath one ceiling, small and cramped, people and machines. Mom was quiet and tired and ready to get some relief from her shallow breath, I was texting my sister to keep her updated on the latest Nurse and Dr. observations.

In walked another nurse. She said hi and began to monitor the readouts from the beeping machines and then she looked hard at Mom and said "I know you". Mom perked up and returned the stare, soon there was this feeling of "ole home week". Mom was talking and Lisa was talking and they were trading notes on who was where and I saw you getting your hair cut by my mom and were you at that church event and those people have moved and that person is living out of state.

I sat in amazement as Mom and Lisa conversed about the people they knew and lived near and I learned all about the latest church and people news. Do you remember that this was all going down in the emergency room?

What had been scary and unknown and hard and uncomfortable and painful was pushed into the background because what was going on was friendly talk and friendly touch and friendly sharing.

I asked myself, do I live in a community where people know me like this? Nope, I do not. When I am in a crowd, I am alone, the hospital near me functions extremely well but when I was there, I didn't see one soul I knew or knew me. I was an unknown and they were unknowns to me. I moved from my childhood community several years ago and moved many times since then, no chance of the kind of depth in relationships my Mom has.

Lisa left to do her duties with other patients and I took notice of the room. It was still. No beeps, dings, blurps, or chimes, nothing but peace, quiet, rest, and a knowing that passes all understanding that everything will be okay.

Mom is home today and doing well. Physically I believe the IVs and tests helped her, but the most important help, LISA, and her connecting with Mom on the deep level of sameness and love.

ENOUGH TO BE DANGEOUS

Back in the early 2000s, I was the novice owner of a commercial carpet cleaning business ready to take on all the dirty carpet in the city.

For years I was hooked on business ownership and dreamed about a business where I was the only owner, the person in charge, the person with all the responsibility and the person who expanded what was to what could be.

My legs were weak and I was scared and nervous and excited.

I didn't have a clue what I was getting into.

I read the latest publications of business books, joined mentor groups, attending networking events and lost a lot of sleep. I knew enough to be dangerous to myself and to employees. What I might have done in those early years is wear a large red sign that said "beware, making changes without understanding consequences".

Early on I discovered that hearing about or reading about business ownership is a heck of a lot different than being there. At the office, in the warehouse, on the parking lot facing employees that were not all that interested in a woman-business owner. They were not sold on the story that I could make this cleaning business more profitable and successful than it currently was. In fact, I met more wariness than confidence in practically every employee.

Book learning and mentor advice has its place. But when it comes down to showing up, I found that there is nothing scarier than putting into practice the lessons from the book pages and from mentor's advice.

Now this is where the rubber met the road. For me it became more action and less talk.

I decided that I wanted to be a different type of owner, and to be different I had to act different from the expected.

I arranged employee focused training and added benefits and upped wages and spotlighted families.

I wanted to prove a point which was this. That I would manage the business, I would handle the good and the not-so-good and I would make a difference.

Fast forward to 2021. This year was a roller-coaster ride with uncertainty and the slowdown of accounts, causing us to scramble to find work to keep us all in the green-stuff.

And we did it. Together, working and planning and being flexible. Focusing our eyes and ears and time on what is important to us.

Never would this have worked out as well as it has if not for years before when employees were spotlighted front and center in the business.

And for that I give thanks.

ERROR HONESTLY MADE

Are you encountering more than usual shortness of patience within yourself and the people you know?

I sure am. In fact, this has been so noticeable to me that I hesitate to ask for an item such as postage stamps, office supplies, or zoom conference team call, because of not wanting the impatient response. Or eye-roll, or ignorement, or slow return. Sound familiar?

This whole mess of impatience came to a head recently when I witnessed a person screaming and carrying on about their phone not working, come to find out it was working, error honestly made, but the guy couldn't figure it out, the remedy he took was screaming and carrying on.

His error of not understanding how the phone functioned created for him an internal storm.

Bingo! I saw myself in that instance. Angry when my computer program would not follow my instructions and do what I tapped it to do. I saw myself in that guy when the line I was in at the grocery store was slower than I thought necessary. I saw myself in that guy while I was fuming about the take-forever line at the airport, waiting to get through security.

How many of these impatient situations were orchestrated because of an error honestly made? The guy with the phone, his error, couldn't figure it out, and very much honestly made. My lack of patience with computer programs, my error for sure, grocery line or airport, I half-believe were human errors honestly made, I didn't wait around to find out.

Since seeing the phone guy episode, I tell myself to take a step back and take a breath when impatience calls my name.

Errors honestly made are still errors, sure. Reactions though might possibly alter when we recognize the error as an honest mistake. It happens all the time, errors made. Honest mistake? More than we probably realize.

EXCELLED AT WHAT SHE DID

I recently read this excelled description in a book and came away with the question. Where is the proof?

Excelled is not a word to throw out randomly. On the contrary, it is a serious word.

"Excel" to surpass others and do exceptionally well. Way out of the ordinary, scads more than was required, overboard in more. (the last three definitions are from Marleen's dictionary).

For reference, I looked around at the activity of people familiar to me who I believe have overcome challenges and stayed true to their commitments. You might be encouraged to say they excelled.

Amanda is sightless and independent.

Carol Ann is a caretaker and dependable.

Lynn, facilitator of medical and physical care.

Jim, program developer of International Studies.

Theresa, getting it right every time, government contracts.

Frank, people.

I brought the excelled story to my attention, and when I did, I saw accomplishments in people close to me that I had glossed over.

Reading about a person who excels is easy. Looking around and discovering the people around me that excel, wow! A valuable exercise is seeing what is right before me.

And the proof? The action of doing it again, over, the second, third, or many times, patience, commitment, pain, loss, love, and caring.

FLY ON THE WALL

More often than not, I get the question/message wrong. Someone asks a question, I respond, and puff, I misunderstood AGAIN! Back and forth, the words stream.

If only I could be the "fly on the wall" and observe how people behave and talk when I am not in the room, I would possibly understand the person's dialogue, frame of reference, questions, and answers.

I think a lack of understanding of other people is a huge detriment. Do you? Do you think you always are right-on about getting the gist of what someone is saying? Do you always know what they mean when they are explaining their stuff?

Today, I am not talking about Spanish to English. No, this is English-to-English speaking.

When was the last time you sent a text, and the receiver totally misunderstood what you texted? Gotcha! It happens all the time, but if we were a "fly on the wall" during private conversations, explanations, business meetings, or family meetings, we would be years ahead in interpreting what is being said and meant. We would have the backstories.

BINGO

But, since I am not a fly on the wall and am too big to make that work, I found a work-around option.

If we listen more intensely and learn to do serious listening with our eyes, ears, and whole body, we can drill down to what the sayer is saying.

So, how does this work in the real world?

In person, we look, watch, are conscious of body language, hear words with inflections and ask for more definition.

On zoom, we follow the rules as in-person and add careful attention to eye movement.

Text and messaging are more mysterious. This is the most difficult for me, and where I mess up when I return a text or message. So, I have begun to wait and reread and reread before I respond. Helps, but hasn't cured me yet of not getting it right.

Because this is important, I keep working on getting better, never perfect, but better than last year.

Seriously, since we cannot be a fly or two on the wall, take heart and apply the suggestions here.

Because, honestly, clear communication changes lives.

FALSE IDENTITY

I stop and take inventory whenever I feel a check or anxiety after a meeting—knowing that after years of business ownership, I still sometimes show up as a false person with a glib personality that pretends to be Marleen.

This false identity of mine reared its head a couple of days ago when I was out with another person making cold calls. We were attempting to place vending machines in facilities that either hadn't had one or were tired of their old machine not working and un-serviced.

But it was not until I got home and reflected on the day that I felt actual anxiousness. Then, looking in the mirror, I looked the same. Who knew?

Bingo. When that happens, I go back and take notes of my day.

We think of false identities at Halloween when masks, capes, and hats are the rage. But, undoubtedly, a falseness of identity appears in professionals.

Not so you say? I have seen in life, people wear masks, and not only on Halloween.

Try this for a day to see if this is a valid statement in your workplace. Write out a short list of colleagues, include yourself, and list job personality because you know them well enough, and your/their private personality.

Job Personality   Private Personality

See any differences?

Are we the same person with identical values at work and play? Do we respond in similar ways, work and play? And do we speak honestly and authentically, work and play?

Your list can be a guiding sign for you.

My anxiety stemmed from presenting a false identity during the drive. I resolved the issue, noted when, where, and why, and committed to "do better."

FAST FORWARD

Whenever making a grocery list, I wanted to "Fast Forward" get it done to where every item was in my refrigerator or on the shelf in the cupboard. However, it was the time between making a list and things stored away that I had come to dread.

I called it wasted time and energy.

Then, I decided that this dreading the grocery store was not a good use of time, and what could be out there to make this work for me. The simple solution is to go to the store, buy the groceries, come home, and put each item away.

Except not quite so simple. My mind does crazy whirls and dips whenever I think about a grocery store. The aisles, rows of stuff, florescent lighting, smells, clutter, cold, hot lanes, noise, time spent when I might be elsewhere.

But it's the food thing and the necessity of eating, I cannot avoid it.

One day, I belabored this with a friend when she said, why not order online and get it delivered. Then, you understand that you will not need to repeat your list on the grocery site file. Instead, just reorder as often as you wish, adding and subtracting items you want.

Today, I believe I could be the next "grocery store, online ordering geek."

Online ordering has set me free to be me.

No longer am I entangled in the dread and imagining fast forward, but instead, the groceries arrive at my door with a slight knock.

I still do the putting away thing, but now it is with a smile and thankfulness to whoever came up with the ingenious way to get the food in the home.

Today is a good day.

FIFTY YEARS IS A LONG TIME

My high school days were so long ago and yet a major determining factor in my future.

And because of that, and I wanted to see friends, I ventured into rural Minnesota last Saturday afternoon to check if memory serves.

And it did. Wonderfully.

I was not planning to attend, it was not convenient when I heard about it, the date and time, plus I had other things to do! But, persuasion and a deep desire to befriend my closest classmates had me driving the distance.

Another hesitation was that I had not participated in school extracurricular activities, and I had not made many close friends, just a few. I was a farm girl who went to school, came home, and did chores. My parents had no patience for us to be away except for classroom study.

I love books, sitting at a student's desk, and the smell of the classroom! I have such good memories; now, I can remember the very people in those classrooms.

A new high school building had been built, and the old one was no longer standing. I felt disconnected from the new until I saw classmates and heard voices. I was back in the high school hallway, hurrying to my next class and trying to keep up with my friend's conversation simultaneously.

I was transported back in time, like a time machine.

We had dinner and a short program about us, this class of 50 years ago. We reunited in that room, a group, a class with a rich history of regionally local people. It was inspiring.

Even though some of us stayed near and some ventured far, on this night, we came back to reignite the oneness and radiance of our collective.

And it was magic.

FREE OF MENTAL HURRY

You may wonder why someone loves life, business, and family and has a fear list.

The truth is, I do. Top of my list is a mental hurry. And because it is a fear, it proves to be destructive energy. So, I continually stare it in the face.

What is on your list? Probably not a mental hurry, but something.

I recently discovered the title mental hurry; I always knew what it was but had not put a name to it. Found it, though, in a book published in the late 1800s. Gee, they had a mental hurry then too!

Sure, my thoughts are continually engaged in doing, listening, telling, or planning, which can be a mental meltdown. Because I sometimes wonder if I missed something. Did someone or some idea or opportunity slip past amid busy thoughts?

And my blood pressure rises.

The key that I know is this; when done in an orderly way, all situations produce harmony inside and out.

My kids tell me, "Mom, you gotta deal," and now is one of those times that I believe I will. I will deal by giving myself a few directed minutes every day to make a list of what I am working on and visualize/a mental picture/see good results. By making a list, my thoughts fall in order and slow down.

What is at the top of your fear list? Mental hurry? Maybe, or something different. No matter, make a list, visualize/mental picture/see good results, and chaos becomes a distant memory.

HOW DO I FIND THE QUIET

My daily life was busy, busy, busy until one day I literally skidded to a stop and asked this ingenious question;

How Do I Find the Quiet?

Every night I lay in bed with my mind buzzing with news, jobs, stuff I forgot to do, round and round until I finally fell asleep, waking up wasn't much better, does everyone wake up with more stuff to think about? That was me. My bold decision was that I was completely done with this round and round thinking because honestly, I knew there was more, and somehow, I knew the more involved getting close and personal with the Quiet.

But first things first and my first was to fight to the death this one BIG complicated belief, which was that I, as a business owner and not just any ole business owner, but a WOMEN-OWNED business owner, (believe me that comes with a load of expectations) has to produce over-the-top outstanding results to be considered among my peers successful.

A small sample of the Cliff Notes on Women-Owned, Better Business Owners

We must look good all the time. We must stand tall with our hands on our hips for photos. We must wear black girl suits with white shirts for all presentations, because golly we have to be taken seriously. We must not show weakness ever! And I mean ever because weakness translates to dumb, not serious, and cannot make a decision.

I was introduced to the world of small business where these Cliff Notes were firmly embedded, Business 101 Class. These rules made Quiet for me difficult because there were SO many "have to" "must-dos" "show ups" to keep track of. One beautiful sunny Tampa day I stood in my office and thought about our customers, the building, the vans, employees, and myself and consciously decided to throw out the Cliff Notes, I then proceeded to do a happy dance!

Today I am curious as to why it took me so long to stand in front of that small office mirror and smile at myself? No worries though, because once I garbage the Cliff Notes and began to live in the Quiet, which was simply giving myself permission to relax and dream and imagine

and accept and wear blue jeans, my business flourished and I slept soundly at night.

The Quiet gives and gives, it is like a hand reaching out to touch and invite and encourage.

HAVING A BAD MONTH.... WHAT IF?

The last month has been trying. Just when I believe the virus tide has turned and people are back in their office, wham. Another delay and more of the same waiting game.

So, when I had lunch with a friend and she mentioned I might try the "what if" questioning of events and outcomes, I thought, what have I got to lose. Any mindset was better than the one I was stuck in at that point.

Here is how this works. First, begin reviewing your calendar. Then, ask yourself "what if" and follow that up with a good and happy outcome for every activity. Not only something that could but dream a little and add a bit of flourish.

Let me provide this example. I own a business in Tampa. Next month we have a lot of pressure washing scheduled. The "what if" I have listed is this. What if the jobs scheduled become regular customers, and what if we hire another technician. What if this is our time to solidify our brand. What if the new sign on the building captures a large media group, and we get outstanding media coverage!

Do I have any idea if these what-ifs may happen? Unfortunately, no. But I know it keeps me open to possibilities that I was closed to before.

My lunch friend recommended that I sit down and write a "what if" list later that day. So, I did. I covered a couple pages of "what ifs." Covering a bunch of interests, both personal and business. And I felt lighter and happier.

Now, for the challenge.

What if every person who reads this post creates a "what if" list. Imagine the feelings of happiness. No one can predict what may transpire.

What if?

HIGH SCHOOL COMMENCEMENT ADDRESS

If I were asked to deliver the commencement message at my high school, it would go something like this.

As far as commencement speeches go, this might be considered non-commencement material. Because telling you that you can go out and change the world or, for that matter, change anyone is not so. I have a different story to tell, and it begins like this.

Take a look around. Can you change the person beside you? Change your parents, friends, siblings, or strangers?

Probably not, but the good news is what you can do. You can grow into the best and brightest version of yourself.

Some of you will go on and attend technical training or study toward a university degree, or you might skip all those classroom hours and find the job that draws you in directly from high school.

Whatever path you take, let's focus on just one thing that everyone can do and be for the next few minutes. So, you, me, and the person beside you, let's talk about being the best version of ourselves.

I grew up on a dairy farm with ten siblings, not far from this high school. We worked early mornings and early evenings on farm stuff during the school year and early mornings to early evenings during the summer. My parents had their hands busy with kids, chores, bills, and getting it all to flow together. When high school graduation day came, they were thrilled since we would then be totally on our own financially and expected to get a job that would pay our way. If we continued to live at home, we paid rent to live there.

I stand here as a mother, grandmother, wife, and business owner. But, today, I am not the same person who sat in one of your chairs but totally and entirely changed.

Maybe you could say it is an inside job.

And that job is the job of becoming the best version of ourselves.

You are the change. You are the future. In the phrases here, you reflect the importance of each of us. Evolution and the future are about people, the individuals that make up our world. And nothing changes before me, and you change and become our best selves.

How to begin.

Why not follow this basic shortlist titled: "becoming my best self."

1. Return calls, emails, and texts within a few minutes, no later than 24 hours.

2. Write personal thank you notes. You know the paper and ink deal that requires a stamp.

3. Live a life of order.

4. Think back to your childhood. When did you feel safe? Then, when times are tough, bring that memory to the forefront, and dwell on the secure feeling.

5. Read or listen to books. Try for a book per month, either from the library, local book store, or online. And do not continually buy your favorite author. Instead, pick new authors with unfamiliar material.

6. Find someone who listens to you, a mentor who is not afraid to challenge you.

I lived poor, and I lived with money. Money is better, I guarantee you. As you make decisions, please keep your dream and vision of your future life focused. It may not happen this month, next year, or in 10 years, but once you have challenged yourself and regularly work at becoming the best version of yourself, the dreams, visions, future hopes, and success show up.

As for your first book read? I recommend buying your copy of "The Alchemist" by Paulo Coelho. And when you need encouragement, another viewpoint, or want to feel good about life, open the book and begin to read.

I wish you love and kindness and to become the best version of yourself! It will take a lifetime.

HOW WISDOM TRUMPS SMART

When I was a student at the local school, I was often referred to as "smart." And why would that be? Looking back through cardboard boxes of school stuff, I achieved the same high marks year after year. Which, I now understand, meant I was smart.

As a young academic, maybe, but as a full-rounded life observer, experienced in all the intelligence necessary to be really "smart" at that young age, I had no clue.

So, here is the dig.

Maybe it could be said that an academic is smart, but it is in the interpretation of what smart is that bears a short discussion.

What smart isn't, though, is wisdom.

Smart can be a term describing academics, farming, finance, really most anything can be called smart with one caveat exception. The emotional and the spiritual. Smart people tend to process information logically, whereas wise people process the emotional, the spiritual, and the subtle side of the logic.

I finally figured out why someone called another "smart" rubbed me the wrong way. I was confusing smart with wise, and I saw my error in doing so.

Today, I hear people label another "smart" and immediately categorize which smart box fits into it. No longer am I confused.

And for wisdom, when one has learned the power of experience, knowledge, and sound judgment along with mental capability, or smart, of how things are accomplished, the outcome?

A competent and trustworthy person.

Powerful.

HIGH CLEANING

is the way to best practices in cleaning and appearance.

High cleaning may be a strange and unfamiliar term for you. Let me explain the meaning.

High cleaning is about scientific methods and common sense. Not rocket science but using scientific knowledge to produce the best outcome possible.

When was the last time someone mentioned science in the same sentence as cleaning?

Last week, last year, or never? Science is possibly the number one factor responsible for excellent outcomes in cleaning carpets, especially when discussing commercial carpets in high trafficked areas. The result will be acceptable only when using the systems and knowledge of high cleaning.

Okay, now what exactly am I talking about in this post? Let me explain further.

We delve into science to understand carpet fiber construction and cleaning solution mixture. However, not everyone has attended the cleaning industry training addressing the importance of what can happen using the wrong cleaning system on high-grade commercial carpets.

There is a right and a wrong way to pull and lift out dirt and soil from carpet fibers. And this is much more than a rug, a bottle, and a machine.

Addressing solution, PH factor, water, and ways to administer all the before mentioned is a balance of science and common sense. Please do not flood the carpet for better results. That is not the way of commercial carpet cleaning!

Common sense, scientific? Maybe. I think so. From experience, I would say that I, along with our carpet cleaning technicians, can address the carpet cleaning system, solution, and best frequency by walking the carpeted area and looking for the signs of wear, soil, and texture.

High cleaning is not a hobby for us at Geyen Group South. However, you understand that cleaning is our livelihood and we take high cleaning seriously. Therefore, you could say we are passionate about the subject.

I will leave you with some simple scientific and common-sense cleaning tips.

Remove spots as soon as seen, blot, do not rub, and vacuum regularly, even daily, in high-traffic areas such as hallways and entry.

A last bit of advice. Always check manufacturer carpet cleaning recommendations and hire a company certified by the Institute of Inspection Cleaning and Restoration Organization. It is the best high cleaning agency in our industry.

HOME SEARCH

A few years ago, my mom called out of the blue and asked me to find her an apartment, she told me that she decided to move. Mom was living in a house with a large yard overlooking a pond that was usually filled with ducks and geese in the summer and ice covered in the winter. It was a peaceful welcoming home, most of the time Mom had friends in and she baked cookies by the dozens, the cinnamon and sugar smells met me every time I walked in. Mom loved that home which is why the call was a surprise. I was thrilled though that she wanted to move.

Lately Mom had been seeing her doctor more often and she sat more than baked, sat more than cleaned and sat more than had company. This was very unusual and out of character, she had me worried. Mom told me that she felt like doing nothing and was ready to move where friends were living just down the hall. She said she saw herself living a smaller life in a one-bedroom apartment giving up driving and some of what she considered her independence. This hurt and yet I was overjoyed that she could be somewhere with oversight and others and a degree of watchfulness.

My first step was to call my sister, Cathy. We talked about Mom's health and where she might feel the happiest. This was a big step as Mom had lived a lifetime in the country, never a town citizen and now we were making plans to uproot her countryness to live side-by-side with new neighbors.

Cathy was up to speed on Mom's health and totally on board with Mom's decision. We wanted to be absolutely sure to find the best facility, we understood we were looking for an assisted living place and not a regular apartment building.

The next week we had 3 appointments. I picked up Cathy and we rode together, talking the whole time about Mom, when to move, how to move, then we moved on to family input, family likes and family dislikes. Lots of talk about family dislikes. (We have 9 siblings).

We arrived through google maps to the first assisted living facility. It was rural and newish. We walked through the open apartment, lunch room and community area and asked zillions of questions of the manager, then we left. I couldn't think as I was walking to the car, a wall of sadness and unbelief and Mom can't live here and tears. Cathy felt the same onslaught of feelings. We figured out that not only was this a new direction for Mom, but it was a new direction for us too and it was hard. We were glad the next facility was 30 minutes away; we needed that time to deal with our initial reactions and feelings. Then we went to the next place and left there at a run. We were stymied. Mom decided to move but these places are not where she is moving to, period.

Cathy couldn't make the last appointment so I went alone. The facility was glorious! The location, administrator and available apartment showed like a sunburst. Talk about dancing for joy, I called Cathy immediately and we talked through the details, then I called Mom and repeated everything I said to Cathy. They both said "take it".

The place is spacious and Mom likes the large windows and that the whole apartment is bright and cheery, the bedroom is just the right size for her furniture and the living room, wow, Mom has her sofa bed there. Her main concern was that she would have a place for family to spend the night. It all works.

Neither Mom or Cathy saw it before move-in day but now, 4 years later, the apartment and next-door friends have brought a ton of happiness and joy and friendship and love to my mom.

I FELT NOT SEEN

I lived a healthy organic life style as a young girl. My family ate fresh vegetables out of our garden, meat and chicken from our own livestock and poultry flock and breathed plenty of fresh air. The bounty of rural life treated us well.

I was this freckled-faced left-handed little girl who resided on a dairy farm with plenty of brothers and sisters. Yet even with all the activity on the farm there were many times I felt alone, not seen, not appreciated and even less important. You see the boys were strong, decisive, physical and got to work outside and were never expected to do inside work which was the cooking, dishes, cleaning or laundry. On a good day I was able to be outside in the sun and weed the garden, feed the animals and as I got older drive the tractor. Still the lines were drawn between girl-work and boy-work.

I was anxious to graduate from the local high school and get a job. Then not too many years later I became a wife and mother with the responsibilities of both. How easily I forgot all about my young childhood since now I was working as hard as I knew to keep the household running. It was an awesome task, exactly what I was trained for as a young girl and one I found to my surprise was not as fulfilling as I imagined. That was a fearsome day because I felt stuck and unhappy and uncertain and a whole bunch of unwanted feelings.

My mind continually ran through this script: I have everything going for me. A husband and kids who I loved with my whole heart. Loved them! And isn't that what a woman's life being all about? Family and home, cooking and cleaning, day in and day out? How could I want anything more? That question haunted me.

First and foremost, I woke up to the fact that loving my family and finding outlets for me to grow into the person I dreamed of becoming can work hand

and hand. This involved moving out of my comfort zone on a weekly basis. I researched books on leadership and business, I attended classes, seminars and found a zillion like-minded people. I joined Toastmasters and met a variety of creative and ageless others who had a rainbow of ideas. This was the beginning of the beginning. Scared, you bet, determined, oh yeah!

I pushed on and am very thankful that my family supported me without a doubt, well maybe there were a few doubts along the way. Starts and stops and more starts.

Today I continue to follow the path of self-education and am fulfilling the dream of becoming a business impresario: one who manages businesses and works with local talented employees.

I AM A POLLYANNA

I read an article in our local paper this week. I was so disgusted when I read about yet another politician using an elected office position to slam, verbally abuse, and cause pain to a staff person. Geez. Enough already!

I pulled the article out from the paper edition and shared it with a couple friends. Asking, who does this today, in the day of voices being heard and abuse awareness like never before? Who does this? More specifically, why and what possible satisfaction comes from denigrating another.

When I look around the coffee shop, I see families and several adults this morning. I hear a baby crying, the coffee machine grinding, the sun is shining, and cars are passing out front. Simple and normal and regular.

So, what's up with verbal abuse and shaming from a superior in a workplace? Who transfers from coffee shop behavior to position abuse? I cannot see this oddity on anyone's face sitting here in the coffee shop.

I am beginning to understand. You see, I am a Pollyanna. A person who believes the best tops everything else, and people really look out for others.

My background, work history, family history, and social history speaks of fairness, honesty, and equality.

There had been no room within me for other ideals until life handed experiences in the courtroom, attorneys, government, and mean people.

Today, my Pollyanna persona is tarnished. And maybe that is a good thing.

I BELONG

For many minutes I sit in my favorite fabric chair and wonder how I got to this exact second in life. And usually, the next thought is, why me? Am I capable, reasonable, worthy, experienced, patient, open, understanding, and sound?

Do I belong?

This belonging notion reared its head during a family zoom session recently.

I have a family with incredible abilities, lifestyles, accomplishments, and memories. Yet, while listening and watching via Zoom, I felt like a shadow in the room, or this case, on the screen. The correct lighting was in place, my face sat in the square screen box, volume was good, so how come the separateness?

Now Zoom is out there in the success of connecting people to people. But it truly cannot take the place of face-to-face presence. Times have been abundant, though, when on a family call that our connections can be considered connections PLUS! We are there, we get it, and we laugh through conversations. We belong.

So why feel the change on the last call?

Belonging is a growth area for me, and since I was born into this family and have a history and memories with each person on the call, I want to dig deep. And plan for the next call.

I will listen and try not to talk too much, feel joy in remembered stories told, and relax in the peace that family relationships offer.

After some time, I fleshed out this: When I allow myself to enter during the call and be vulnerable and extend this courtesy to others, I then belong.

To belong and rest in that feeling comforts me.

I HAVE AN IDEA

Whenever I begin a staff meeting with, I HAVE AN IDEA I see eyes roll, it's a sign that my audience has heard this before and the results may not have worked out.

This time though, I do have an original idea and the jury is out if it is a thumbs up or thumbs down. First, though I want to talk about the idea.

I have a background in writing professional emails and industry informational materials, 20 years at least or maybe more. This was when business writing consisted of a single typewritten sheet of white 20lb typing paper, printed out then folded and inserted into a long white envelope next a white sticky address label was attached to the front middle. Add a stamp and drop it into the large blue box to send by snail mail.

That is some background to say I worked hard at composing these letters and paying particular attention to the reader's problem which would be solved if the reader would hire my company. The letter was two short paragraphs with a personal hand signature.

Fast forward to 2021 and I question what I see as the obvious; poor connection with professionals by email. Since email is considered the gold standard and king of communication therein lies a disconnect somewhere.

I began to explore how to change this disconnect and during this same time-frame I took two creative workshops, Storytelling Workshop and Creatives Workshop, and have excitedly come up with I HAVE AN IDEA.

My hypothesis is this: emails sent to professionals can be useful, informative, welcome and also be creative and fill our basic human desire of connection.

Today writing is different than it was 20 years ago. Then a service business laid out the service provided and the prospective company called to ask about pricing. Now with many emails flying into inboxes, it's like overwhelm and attention disorder and who has time for all of this? Hence my hypothesis; repeated here in a different way, if we write to introduce our service to professional people who are either working in their office or at home, we must show up in a human interaction liking way. Simply: let's just be people who like other people and want what is best for them, their company, and their community. Let's cause connection everywhere we write.

Last week I began by writing a sample email (keep in mind what I plan to achieve) every day and posting it on my Creative Workshop site to get feedback from other Creative Work shoppers and see what flies. I write with intentionality and originality focusing on the professionals who will be reading these and keeping it human and creative and connecting and generous.

Yes, I want more business accounts. But first I want email receivers to know that my business consists of people who are caring and real and I believe then and only then will new accounts join us in the service we offer.

The jury is out as I create the emails and begin sending them to prospective customers next month, but this I know, Professionals deserve better than the advertising, complicated, and attention draining emails they are receiving in their daily inbox.

I aim to change that.

I WANT TO DO BUSINESS WITH YOU

I drive the most amazing vehicle. It gets me where I want to go during sun, rain, snow and cold weather. So, when I saw the air leak going on in the back tire I was panicked.

Will I get to the auto repair shop before the whole tire sinks to the asphalt? Or will I hear a thump-thump and ruin the tire before I get there?

I made it.

I had called before I left my office and told the person on the other end of the phone about the tire slowly deflating. I wanted to be sure they would be ready to do the repair when I arrived.

You can imagine my surprise when I walked in to the service area and found 5 blue uniformed service attendants, 1 taking care of a customer and the others either sitting behind their high-top desks or talking with one another. No one looked up, I wandered around making sure someone saw me waiting, still no eye contact. Shoot, I wanted to do business with this auto repair place, but they were making it hard.

It took some patience on my part, when finally, someone asked me if she could help me, I relayed the tire loosing air problem, she took a look and estimated a longer repair time than anticipated. I scheduled an Uber to give me a lift home. Oh, and by the way, the service person had not known that I had called in for the appointment and that I had already gone over that the almost flat tire needed to be repaired.

I left unimpressed. Later when having coffee and meeting with a colleague, he shared a similar service story, or rather non-service, with a service company, only his frustration was with the lack of care, listening or understanding the issue which he was sharing by a phone call.

Listen everyone working in a service business: Many People Want To Work With You and Do Business With You and Refer You.

But you make it hard for us, your customers or potential customers to do so.

This is serious for me. I own two service-based businesses, the amount of undependable service I see in the workplace speaks directly to my heart. This has to change, people.

Let's not drop the ball and lose our focus. Service First, Money Follows.

I WAS IN AN ACCIDENT

I was driving from a favorite coffee shop to my office when during a turn from one street to another a motorcycle collided with the side of my van. The noise of metal grinding again metal, the push of weight against the van, and the stillness afterward was alarming. I braked immediately, not knowing what hit me, and when I stepped out of the van, I was horrified to see a motorcycle on its side in the middle of the intersection. My heart pounded erratically, my legs shook and I was stunned.

The driver was sitting on the pavement and my first thought was to thank God. Emergency help arrived soon after doing what they do and we were all released.

I filed the accident report with proper insurance protocol and since my van was undrivable and unrepairable I dealt with loss reporting.

Not long after submitting the accident report, my life became more complicated. My insurance company refused to pay the motorcycle guy's damages, while I agreed with their decision, I also believed unfortunately they had to take the hit. The other driver wasn't insured.

So now we were in a tug-of-war and a lawsuit was filed. The motorcycle driver became the Plaintiff and I and my company the Defendants. I hadn't been in an accident before so this was an initiation in lawsuits and legal actions.

Attorneys on both sides set up the case. I was confident with the 2 attorneys representing my interests, they had solid experience and plenty of legalese to represent this case and defend my involvement and responsibility. I trusted them. We spent a fair amount of time back and forth discussing details and strategy and position and what it all means and timeline and more legalese about the case.

After 2 years the case came to trial. By now I felt like I was on a first-name basis with the legal system. The trial was serious, nerve-wracking, and frightening. It lasted all day.

I felt a disproportionate amount of angst and drama and misrepresentative of the facts presented by the Plaintiff's attorney. He took dramatic storytelling to the max as he misrepresented the details of the case. I sat in amazement and disgust as both witness and officer from the accident scene were questioned. It was unbelievable to me that this style of attorney behavior was allowed in a real court of law and both women caved beneath the intensity of the moment.

This was a new life experience and even though I wanted to bail, I had to stay in the boat and ride it down the rapids. The stage was set and the attorneys were front and center. I felt like a fly being batted back and forth. This way and that, when finally, the truth of having no control over the situation surfaced in my mind and I relaxed into my chair and watched.

I left the downtown office building early that evening located my car in the nearby parking garage and drove straight to my apartment where I sank onto my bed as the events of the day played out in my head again and again. My body felt heavy, sedated, and energy less. I was overwhelmed with the many words thrown around during the trial. Not facts mind you but story-telling of what might have could have or should have occurred. My mind was like pizza with all the toppings. A mess of words. And my heart, it hurt.

The following week the judge's verdict was handed down and not long after the lawsuit was settled.

As I searched for closure, I vacillated between two extremes until I realized there aren't two extremes.

Our justice system isn't black or white, fair or unfair, yes or no. It is gray and grayer, red and redder, black and blacker. This realization of what is instead of dreaming about what might be helped me accept the entire legal process.

Today if I were to address my legal experience in a word it would be:

TEACHABLE and LONELY (okay, that's 2 words)

IF NOT NOW, WHEN

A good friend texted me that we should get together when I am back in town. Period. End of text.

I was left with the question of which one of us inks the calendar and makes the initial contact to ensure this happens?

This got me thinking. If not now, when? A friends' text to plan a coffee is a small event. What about something more significant, like hiring a staff person, working with a new vendor, buying a small business, or moving to a more convenient location?

My brain seems to move in different directions. First, it says let's do it and commit to begin the journey of change. Then, a short time later, I find myself digging out the latest and most fantastic read and paging to where I left off.

Later. There is always a later to do the other stuff.

Last month my avoidance habit became glaringly apparent and stopped me in my tracks. What was I doing to get from here to where I knew, absolutely knew, I needed to be? So, I grabbed a blue pen and wrote down a few committed changes to work on in the next few months. And today, I am doing the work to get in the game and cause change to happen.

If not now? When?

IN A FIGHT WITH GOOD

WHEN A HIRE DOESN'T WORK OUT

I work in the commercial carpet cleaning industry as the business owner of a small company. When I began this work/job/owner position in Tampa, I inherited a staff of people who neither knew me, liked me, or respected me. A challenge for sure but one I was up for. The business was unfamiliar and I set myself up to be a quick study, I understood the industry and I had the experience but I was unaccustomed to guys who worked on an hourly basis with different equipment and most certainly in a different climate.

I struggled through a few years of employee management while at the same time was furiously reading management materials and joining business organizations, networking with higher-ups, middles, and lower-downs, and plainly I was out in the business community talking to many professionals who had experience and were open to give advice. I felt it was vital to understand the people who worked with me. Clearly, I also was giving myself a few kudos as the business grew and more staff was hired.

But one day it all fell apart.

There was this employee who insisted on only driving his favorite company van, he claimed it was his and he refused to change even though this wasn't making a whole lot of business sense I had discussed with him his complaints and unhappiness going so far as to ask him to look for employment elsewhere since he obviously wasn't settled in his current job. I offered to help him begin his own small residential business but nothing I volunteered turned out to be a career change he wanted.

On this day, he pushed too far in his loud angry voice and I felt threatened and afraid for my business. As far as I was concerned, he sealed his un-employment with me. I called the police and asked for an off-duty person who would meet me at the office and be there while I did the hateful job of firing an employee. I also requested that this someone be big, tall, in uniform, and carrying a gun. It was arranged and I explained my plan and what turned out to be the best way to handle it with the least negative reaction.

The security person sat and witnessed the difficult, direct and final conversation, and yes, he was big, tall, in uniform, and carried. My hope was that this would be a peaceful event, but I couldn't be sure, hence the security precaution which gave me the confidence to do it and get it over with.

As it turned out I fired him that afternoon and he walked out still complaining and in plain sight of all the other employees, they stood by in silence.

During this tough and long 30 minutes, so many emotions rose up and I asked myself over and over the same question: could I have handled it differently?

But when Manny, one of the guys watching this firing in real-time, walked over, looked me in the eye, smiled, and said "you did the right thing here, no one else will make the mistake of not taking you seriously they now respect you". My heart began beating again.

Manny gave me a gift that afternoon.

INSURANCE MADE SIMPLE

I am not an insurance person, agent, adjuster, or broker. What I have experienced is the interaction that happens because of accidents. I am talking about a company driver, police, on-lookers, attorneys, and insurance.

When you are a small business owner in Tampa, accidents are a fact of business life.

You might even consider me an almost expert in the field.

A few Saturdays ago, the commercial carpet cleaning at an account 15 miles away was arranged. Unfortunately, while in route, an accident involving our company van, two technicians, and the driver of another other vehicle occurred...

A driver without insurance. A driver who freely admitted, "my brakes don't work." Which made perfect sense since this person rear-ended the company van at a stop.

Do I turn this into insurance? Absolutely no! And this decision will not change no matter how much damage our van has because insurance, at least here in Florida, is about protecting other drivers. Other drivers willingly sue business owners because, they can.

This last year we experienced an unusually high occurrence of fender benders to company vehicles. And these fender benders range from rear-end, backside, and back wheel collusions. What a way to spend insurance dollars!

Only, we don't! We do not use insurance funds to do our repairs. We absorb the costs. And do much of the repairs in-house.

Insurance dollars are for the other driver, the driver who wants money to cover repairs, and the lofty idea of fairness.

I learned from reports that fault does not often lie with our drivers. Sure, we make mistakes, but lately, it has been a matter of being in front of a driver who made a wrong decision.

The simple truth is that business insurance money is about paying out to the other drivers and not paying to loyal contract insurance holders. And I pay strict attention to that policy, which I learned through painful discussions with insurance adjusters.

Once I understood business insurance, I slept better and had no more worries about what if, what how, and what cost. The formula is this simple.

Owner Business Insurance = pay for the other driver, not associated with the business.

You may ask, why continue in small business with these escalating and out-of-control costs?

Crazy, I guess!

IT HAPPENS DOWN THE STREET

It happens down the street, divorce, jail sentence, death from cancer, auto accident, alcohol, drugs, sickness ……. until it doesn't.

We might say not in my family, nope, not in the cards. Only for a stranger, neighbor, friend, siblings, but mine?

We like to think these terrible happenings cannot possibly touch us in that very up-close and personal way.

My initial response when someone I knew had a death in their family or a serious illness was "how can I help" until a friend of mine, who lost a young daughter to cancer said, "Marleen, we don't know what help we need because we are in so much pain". It's better to offer a few things you can do such as I can be there for……. I can manage the food and calls; I can keep the cleaning or dog-sitting in check.

Oh, and don't call this divorce, court decision, death a "life-changing event" PLEASE! Life-changing, absolutely! But the term has been wrung out and diluted by the media these days.

Not all that long ago it happens down the street became it happens in our home.

No notice or forewarning or video/preview for preparation.

I had checked my rental car at the airport and shortly before the flight as I was standing in the terminal, my husband called to "let me know". I walked over to the nearest wall, slid down, and sat on the floor, totally oblivious to all activity around me. A fog descended, completely encompassing my body and I sat.

Fast forward.

Since the day of reckoning, that what happens down the street ALSO happens in my family, I feel other people's pain more. By more I mean, up close, in my body, on my skin, and I work tremendously hard to be aware and open and cautiously helpful when I find out someone is faced with a terrible and difficult situation.

It happens down the street also happens in my home.

IT IS ALL ABOUT ME

It might be because I have a slew of family, cousins, nieces, and nephews that I was taught to always put another person first. As a result, and since all social gatherings were crowded being first in anything was a moot point.

It was not unusual for me to extend an invitation to the person next to me to step in front at the meal line, settle in the middle seat in the car, or show up as johnny-on-the-spot for dirty dish detail and laundry and cleaning and babysitting.

You get the idea. I was acting out within ingrained habits without thinking about what I was doing. I became a non-self with no room for me, and questions and creativity and openness and dreaming and wanting and...... I brought these "follow along" habits with me into adulthood.

Then one day, when I was old, I looked at my actions, primarily my efforts within a group, and decided I was not all that happy with that version of Marleen.

And so, I changed. Slowly at first, I gained confidence and momentum.

Do you know that you attract happiness when you show up as yourself? I discovered that first-hand.

My life is healthier today. This is because I no longer wait for someone to step in with new ways of doing things so I can follow along.

No more waiting for someone, anyone, or the right person to step up with questions or solutions.

You might say I fired the old Marleen and hired this new version of me.

Your new version is available if you want it. A unique and different version of one-self, just in case the old version is not working out so well.

Let's draw back the curtain of a new one-act play. A play with new stars! And the title?

It Is All About Me.

IT'S ALL A MIND GAME

I have a vending customer who moseys around and shows up in the break room every time we are there to load the machine. Every Time. He stands, looks, and assumes I will hand a complimentary beverage to him.

How do I know this? At the start of our relationship, every single conversation was about price—every conversation. Then, while we were there managing and activating the machine, he stepped in to look.

We were blissfully happy to get the items on the correct shelves and the cash/credit card apparatus working.

"How about a beverage," he asked with expectation. He was insinuating that it was "free for him."

This became a mind game.

And we were attuned from the get-go. Decision time. Should we stop and point or tag along and let it ride?

We asked each other if we should address it with this guy or play along.

And then, we asked a few qualifying questions, such as: What is the cost to the business and our future relationship? And since it was about something other than the money (not very expensive handing over a coke), we agreed to ignore it and keep the relationship intact.

I encourage you to look at business relationships, hierarchies, titles, wage differences, and expectations. Are games being played?

It would be healthier if these games became open conversations, but that is sometimes impossible.

Maybe, just maybe, a future training catalog will differentiate itself by offering a degree titled:

"Mind Games Played in Business."

We can relate!

JURY SUMMONS AND RELIEF

I was notified to serve my responsibility for jury duty. This was new for me and my first time ever. So, I crafted lots of ideas on how I would answer probing questions about my personal beliefs. Because I thought that was the type of questions asked before you get the green light to sit in the powerful jury box.

I was not very happy with our legal system. In my experience with depositions and court appearances, the system I imagined and the system I experienced was unlike one another. As a result, I was angry and disappointed with the courts in general.

But from the time I received the notice to the actual morning of appearing in the courthouse, life had happened. New changes in daily activity in both my business and in my personal life. From summons to the courthouse, I had changed because real life, living, changes us.

After a few weeks went by, it was too much effort to float up the past anger. Too much wasted energy. Too much bringing back the past.

I arrived at the 8:00am hour at the courthouse and walked through security and up the stairs. I entered the waiting room for jurors. I immediately appreciated the clean carpet and padded chairs until the thought passed my mind of the need for padded chairs because the wait time was so long. Not so pleased now.

There were around fifty other adults in the room. Most on their phones, me, reading a book, all listening for further directions from the court.

I felt committed to sitting for jury duty while at the same time I knew I would be relieved if I was not selected. Gone was any thought of wanting an attorney audience to voice past history.

And then surprise! After 55 minutes of waiting, a kind woman's voice came over the speaker to say that the sitting judge no longer required jurors. Oh, Happy Day!

Smiles were everywhere as we filed out of the room. I guess I was not the only possible juror who had other plans.

As far as the earlier anger and the vital need to tell my story, all gone. When I decided to drop it, it fell. Oh, Happy Day!

LANGUAGE BEHIND THE WORDS

Lately, I see the word "woke" printed everywhere. He is woke, she is woke, am I woke? So, I began a mission to understand the language behind the word and its meaning. Unfortunately, this woke word seemed to be yet another buzzword, and I am attempting to eliminate all buzzwords in my writing and speech thoroughly.

Can anyone write too much about cancer, memory loss, alcoholism, happiness, divorce, or living a human life? I don't think so. When we write, and when we read, the writer's intention shows up on our faces. The language and feelings behind these words show up within and spill over to facial movement.

So, then there is this word, woke. The online dictionary ap I refer to posts that woke means active awareness of injustices, prejudices, and understanding of facts, and what happens after consuming lots of coffee. So, I understand the last definition.

I think the word sounds funny. It is descriptive and tends to feel like a buzzword that impresses instead of defining or clarifying. Maybe I am wrong, but when I am in an audience of suit-wearing individuals, I guess "woke" works in language usage and understanding (it IS the word of the hour). Still, not everyone I meet and converse with is in the suit-wearing career, and using a new word to talk about prejudice and injustice seems like overkill.

Instead of adding definition and language, we add another layer of "the latest coolest, most hip word." By saying woke within the conversation, we attempt to appear that we are in the know and with it.

What a bunch of nonsense.

As I write about human connection and business, I promise to continue to do so with as much clarity and honesty as possible.

LANGUAGES WE SPEAK

The first time I drove in New York City I was 19 and scared out of my mind! Here was this Minnesota girl steering her green nova through streets that were unfamiliar and had me feeling like I was in a foreign country.

I wanted to see New York City since I was a little girl and I was determined that given the chance, I would take it. The chance came and I took it.

Never thinking that a snowstorm would arrive the day before my arrival to the city, I hadn't planned for it and surely didn't consider the consequences.

Driving and totally lost I found my way to a gas station to ask for directions, the guy answered my questions but I couldn't understand a word he said. I was totally out of my element, when I got back to my car, I was now lost both in the city and lost in my thoughts.

I stopped a few more times to ask for directions, again no understanding of the answers given. What?

You see, I figured out that I was in Brooklyn and these guys were speaking Brooklyn English to my Minnesota English. This was my first experience with language that didn't make a lick of sense to me. Never before had I had the chance to get out of dodge, and when I did, I found myself in a place where English was not the language, I thought it was.

Remember it had just snowed a bunch, the streets were packed with snow, cars, and me. I was freaking out for a time and directionless until I stopped, took many breaths and looked around, took my time, and miraculously found my way out of a city I had only dreamt about. I made it! I was there and I survived.

LISTEN WITHOUT COMMENT

Not being heard is a small business owner's nightmare. Ugh. Especially when a part of the job is to manage others within the company and those same "others" are not listening.

Employees also find not being heard true. Who does not want to work with a manager that listens first, without comment, before making a final determination? No-one.

In professional office buildings, small black security cameras mounted on office walls and ceilings throughout a building and throughout the parking garage tell a story. For example, as my carpet cleaning technicians do their work, these cameras continually record their physical activity. In real-time, every footfall, and every movement.

We can and do receive calls periodically from account managers who have watched the security tapes from the previous day or night. They check in with us about adding more carpeted areas or asking questions about systems, or sending their thanks to our techs for a job well done.

If we receive a call from an account contact saying something like, "your guys were goofing around last night on the job," we take it seriously. On the one hand, I honestly want to respond, "does the carpet look good, and was the job completed as scheduled, because that is what you hired us to do. And FYI, the guys who work with me are professionals; they are certified and trained in commercial carpet cleaning. They are working throughout the evening and night to do the best cleaning your carpet can have. And another thing, when the service is delivered, as guaranteed it would be, the behavior of my technicians is none, do you hear me, none, of your concern!

That is what I want to say, but thankfully I do not.

Instead, it goes something like this. "Thanks for your report. We will check it out and be sure it does not happen again." The customer is always right. How do we handle this?

And then, I sit with the technicians from the carpet cleaning job and ask what happened. Because you see, it is crazy easy to jump to conclusions and want to reprimand and lecture and list consequences, but thankfully I do not. I sit, and I listen.

And here is what I have learned from seasoned experience; by asking questions and listening first to employees before commenting right, wrong, or in between, I get the whole picture of the episode.

Nine times out of 10, once the guys explain what went on in the building, with the carpet, with the security person, with somebody still at work at their desk, and even with a phone charging, I understand why they acted the way they did while on the job. I also appreciate the inaccurate interpretation of the account contact viewing the security tape.

We have found from back-and-forth discussions that the most challenging part of the technician's job position is letting go of unnecessary comments made by security officers and people on-site who do not understand how we do our work. Therefore, we thoughtfully created a training outline presented at our scheduled training meetings; we talk about the best way to politely respond to on-site questions, relax body language and work with security personnel.

I believe the old-school quote that the customer is always right is just that, old-school. However, years and experience in customer service have shown me that the customer often is not correct. And may not know the whole story and is unwilling to listen without commenting, so our response continually is, thank you, we will take care of it. We follow through with communication with our staff.

As for the technicians goofing around at the job site that night, as I listened without comment when they reasonably explained their actions, they were justified, and I heard them.

LOOKING FOR VALUE INNOVATION

I saw the phrase in a book I am reading, Value Innovation, which by the way, directly from the author, means lowering cost while increasing value.

How is a conscientious business doing that? It depends.

I had a Calendly meeting this morning with a great guy. He stands up for a company that schedules appointments. Brice knew his service product and outlined how the program flows. In the back of my mind, I kept thinking about value innovation and how we could deliver more value at less cost. And might Brice's appointment people be an excellent fix to appointment setting? Would Brice's staff add value innovation to our business? Remember, this translates as low cost + increased value.

To be transparent, I created a filter questionnaire. And before making strategic business decisions, or any decisions for that matter, the idea, suggestion, or opportunity filters through a value innovation questionnaire.

Are you somewhat confused about what makes up Value Innovation?

Let's look at this from a personal human relationship.

My daughter texted to see if I was free to meet her for breakfast. Usually, we meet at a well-known and familiar place for breakfast. But on this day, she suggested a new venue.

No one was at the front door to let us in, so our 9a time was pushed back—a snaggle and disappointment.

But the food! Wow!

My daughter and I discussed what worked in determining value innovation about our breakfast. We analyzed the waiter, table, water, location, and menu selection.

Value Innovation lower costs while increasing value. Costs can show up in several ways: food, drink, more gas, time, and tip.

We agreed on the meal quality, seating, and service. And our collective value innovation was lower cost and increased value. To prove that, we have already set our next breakfast date and time.

Let us go back to business.

Who isn't looking at an upswing in value innovation? No one I know.

And the book? BLUE OCEAN SHIFT, Beyond Competing, by W. Chan Kim and Renee Mauborgne

LUNCH WITH LUCY

I was spending time with a staff person the other day, and when we parted, I could not remember what our conversation centered around.

I abruptly caught myself and realized this, and it scared me.

I was so not present that I had not even engaged.

There were no excuses, especially from me.

I blew it.

Employee engagement is never far from my definition of a successful business. I have created educational presentations, hired trained presenters, given away books, arranged lunch meetings, dinner meetings, an employee of the month, but today it seems we are in the mully-grubs, and it begins with me.

Last week, I ran across the book "Lunch with Lucy" out of the blue at the airport bookstore. What timing! I was looking for an original "game plan."

It seems like we are suffering from the blahs after months of unhappy, uninspiring, fear-producing media, and I think we are looking like robots programmed to keep on walking.

Hence, this book appeared at just the right time, for the right price, and it had my undivided attention on a 3-hour flight.

Spoiler Alert: I am somewhat hesitant reading "investing in your people" books. In the past, I found lots of advice written for employees born or acclimated to our American workplace. However, in my business, it is a different story.

We are a small service company with diverse backgrounds, and we came here from various countries. English is not our first language. Not just the normal "are you from Florida or Minnesota, Wisconsin or New York"? (Okay, New York and Wisconsin? Different countries)

The book is a show-stopper. After a few chapters, I wrote down a couple of suggestions on alignment and engagement.

Today a few shifts are in the works, just simple tweaks, not a complete over-haul. Keeping track and 100 percent sure employees are rightfully front and center.

As for Results, Improvements, Satisfaction? Patience, and wait and see.

2022 looks like a turn-around year; it's in the stars!   i.e.: Employee Stars.

MANAGEMENT BY EXPERIENCE

I have to be honest; I have a drill Sargent personality. I wasn't all that aware of it since the kids have grown up and gone off on their own until recently when my granddaughter began to salute as she was hurrying out to the car to get in and accompany me on an errand. In my head I said "darn, it is still there".

At work, a continual annoyance of little things bothered me and I found myself repeating bad words in my head, words my mother didn't allow said in the house when I was a little girl.

After a few actions from employees that were no-no's in the handbook such as wearing part of our service uniform, shirt but forgetting the pants or wearing the pants and not the company logoed shirt I knew I had to address the issues. But even when I was seeing the small hiccups, I didn't want to rock the boat and draw attention.

I found myself wondering how can a drill Sargent personality such as mine not want rules to be followed? I dislike confrontation when it involves my work and professional life but as far as giving orders to family members I know and love no problem.

I wanted to get this under control, the actions of a few employees, and the best way to address it in a workable way. This was a learning and implementing step for me. I read a bunch of positive books on professional management and then took my husband's advice and tossed most and came up with my own version of committed management. Here is what it looks like today.

I want everyone on staff to have the freedom to make decisions based on experience and knowledge and common sense. I also trust that every one of us has a comfortable and friendly relationship with the people we work with.

To put my words into action I schedule myself to lead a few training sessions and talk about the specifics of management and how interaction among ourselves plays out in the workplace.

Put another way, during these sessions I talk about the little things we do, why uniforms, critical conversations, body language, tone of voice, and I ask questions and ask more questions and then I listen. My greatest understandings as a business owner have been during these training sessions which always close with questions, responses, inquiries, and decisions made.

As far as Sargent behavior? Haven't seen it show up for a long time, which leads me to believe it has retired with no benefits.

MARY'S DAY CHANGES

The call came in the middle of the night. The voice was frantic and worried and sharp.

By listening to the voice message, I could tell that this was an urgent matter. Good thing she left her name and number. Mary, XXX.XXX.XXXX

Usually, Mary's every day office life was quiet and normal. Each day was like the next, no noticeable changes, in at 8a and out by 5p. Just another workday until that email arrived in Mary's inbox just before sunset while Mary was outside on her patio.

First you must understand, Mary's job is to manage an entire floor of small individual offices in an office building next to the airport. That's 25,000 square feet of carpeted space. Desks, tables, cabinets, chairs, sofas, on and on, all office stuff that filled every available square foot.

But the email changed the everyday-ness of Mary's work day. Here is how It read in 12pt bold print, "Hello Mary, all old office furniture on the north side of the building is being moved out and new reconditioned office furniture is being delivered next week, make it happen".

Mary's first thought "make it happen?" then "what's in the frig for dinner".

Where do I begin and immediate action is required and it best be immediate to get the job done by the deadline. I haven't done this before and for sure not on this short rope of time. Who do I ask? I need help! Are emails or texts the best way to reach out or maybe a phone call?

Hence the voice message in the middle of the night on my business line. Mary and I have a professional friendship, we worked together on a project in her office last year and then repeated the same project this year. I replayed the message a few times to be sure I got the gist and urgency of the call.

I returned Mary's phone call at 7:30 am thinking she may already be in her office. She was busy at her list making and adamant to find out the exact move day. Her voice sounded anxious and from the traffic noise in the background, I believe she was just getting out of her car. We talked about what needs to happen and when so the project stays on schedule and I volunteered to call a few people I work with on projects and get the ball rolling. I called, emailed and texted, cc'ing Mary on every note, to be sure the message was transferred in the right manner. By evening, Mary had her plan in motion, she had met with everyone who had a stake in the moving project and was ready to move forward on the timeline. She said she felt ready.

So, the days went by and the list became shorter as Mary inked off items as they were done. I checked in with her daily and was delighted to hear her talk about the project and how well it was coming together, the furniture looked perfect for the office, even the people officing on the south side liked the look, bright greens, bold reds and hip.

The deadline was met and Mary well satisfied as she walked down the hall and peaked in offices outfitted with new reconditioned furniture.

Since she is a hands-on manager and worked alongside everyone, Mary told me she had a reason to wear her favorite washed-out jeans, I-am-SuperWoman T-shirt and crocs to work all week! Extra bonus! This was a short notice job that she aced which will certainly help her in the job review coming up and super important is Mary's deep confidence in her abilities and new professional friends she can honestly refer to others.

Mary and I walked through the north side offices together a few weeks later and the change was dramatic. No more dull colors, Mary said that she feels her spirit lift every time she has a reason to check out these offices and as for leasing each one? It's a piece of cake.

MEDIA SOAKED

Not too long ago I wasn't too happy with the outcomes in my life and I continually felt that I was being pulled and pushed in a way that I didn't like. What is the wisdom quote "you are what you read, watch and listen to". Once I stopped to think about where this not-good feeling stemmed from, I was sure this saying applied to me.

The straw that broke the camel's back though was when

I read a post written by a person I admired, she was a friend, but after reading her post I immediately felt a negative

judgment towards her and added to the judgment was a few unkind words. This had to stop. I had to do something now not waiting until next week.

So, I changed my news access direction to not-often and stopped a few online daily reads and researched a few new ones. I wanted to be a kinder and more compassionate person and to do this I knew I had to remove and replace the information I was accessing in the areas of reading, watching, and listening.

Would I miss the big events on the horizon, would I miss not seeing the daily updates on news sites where I was a r. I was 100% unsure how my keeping-up-to-date self would like this.

Would I become an unenlightened citizen and blind to the universe I lived in? Or worse would I be LABELED UNINFORMED! Yikes, that was scary.

I began reading genres that I hadn't before. I met authors through new books and new blogs that were upbeat and focused on the good and great and growth in life. It was invigorating!

I took a class online then another right after finishing the first and found new friends in Spain, Argentina, and Scotland. We talked about where we were going and how we were getting there. Future plans and learning more and doing more and seeing more and just plain more! It was like a MORE CLASS! Exhilarating and refreshing. I forgot about where I had been a couple months before in my funk and judgment-filled life, now I didn't have time to do the judgment thing, too much other new work in progress.

A few months sailed along and much to my surprise I found decision-making easier and more effective with the people I work with and with my family and friends.

My countenance became relaxed and calm and happy. Did I realize the effect I have on others? I don't think I did at least not to the degree I understand it now. When I am me, and you are you, when we are working and finding our work pleasing, our bodies show it.

My audience is the people who see me, your audience is the people who see you. What do you think your audience is saying about you? We are what we "read, watch and listen to" that is unarguably true. Once I re-grabbed that again and got it, I changed what I read, watched, and listened to.

MIXING WOMANHOOD WITH

BUSINESS HOOD

Last week my mother entered a hospice program, and the next day a daughter-in-law gave birth. Mixing womanhood with business hood at this most intimate level left nothing within me but gratitude. Gratitude that this is my life, the life I chose and am now able to live, to help my mom out of bed and encourage a new mother to welcome her newborn.

Previously I would isolate mom-caring from significant business demands, but last week, the flood of family decisions to be made over-ruled. I got it done by holding a phone in one hand and responding to a business email with the other. It was complicated. It was hard. It was what daughters do with and for their aging mothers.

Awareness and reverence and wonder and miraculous and happy and concerned and focused and incredibly loads to feel.

My mom with breath, presence, movement, smile, and need. She needs us, her family, at this most critical life juncture.

As I sat at the small kitchen table, I realized we needed Mom. Her being, her soft voice, her reassurance that this is her time.

This new mother is overcome with the miracle of her fragile baby, love, care, and enchantment. She is now sharing the just born grandchild through Face-Time with a great-grandmother.

Womanhood and Business hood, not one or the other but both. Both during hard, emotional times, both during happy family celebrations, both during the day-to-day activity of life.

Womanhood and Business hood, not one or the other but both during the cycles of life.

MOM I MISS YOU

Every day since Mom has passed, I miss her. Mom is at the top each morning when I write my gratitude list.

Why?

This is a puzzle. Yes, I spent many hours with Mom, especially the last few years of her life, but she was 95 years old! For goodness' sake! And ready to pass. Mom often spoke about her passing and legacy. She remarked many times that she had no regrets.

So why the daily remembering and missing? It has been over a year since she left us.

I thought I was prepared for the final goodbye, but I was not.

I keep memories of living at home on the farm close to my heart. Sunday afternoons and hours of swinging. The unforgettable smell of freshly mown hay and the jingle of cow chains. Then my teenage years of begging for the use of the car, asking to stay out late, and sneaking a drink or three.

In my memories of Mom, she shows up as a stern decision-maker, unafraid of conflict with one of her kids. You could say, a disciplined taskmaster who leads by example, for which I am forever grateful.

Then in my adult years, I forgot about Mom most of the time, busy living apart, creating a family, and working at a business. I was waist-deep in responsibilities and commitments, setting aside no time to spend with Mom. Reminds me of that song by Harry Chapin, Cat's in the Cradle,". Paraphrased, "when you coming home, daughter," I don't know when, but we will get together then." Yeah, me.

And this morning? I miss my mom.

I aged, she aged, and as her physical needs increased, I stepped up. This may be selective memory, but the past no-seeing-mom years got foggy, and the days spent with Mom shined the brightest. We talked, laughed, and decided things. It was marvelous!

Today the feeling of "missing Mom" confuses me. I had time with her. I said everything I wanted to say, she talked and thanked me. And when we said all there was to say, we sat together, just being in one another's space. It was marvelous.

But I miss her. She feels close but not here! I wish she was in her apartment having coffee with friends, hosting Bible Study, and making friends with strangers at the store. But that is not so.

Mom, I had no idea I would miss you so much. It does not hurt. It's more like I want you here, so my life feels whole. I did not think the change would be so front and center when you passed, but it is.

MOTORCYCLE LICENSE OR BUST

The challenge of getting a motorcycle license was always a pie in the sky idea until I attended a networking event at the local Harley Davidson dealer where I checked out the bikes, walked around, and dreamt of what it must feel like to drive one.

Driving a motorcycle frightened me, ever since I laid my brother's bike down on a highway when I was a teenager, didn't get hurt but it freaked me out.

And here I was at a dealer thinking about that fear and decided enough of that and signed up that very night for classes to get my motorcycle driver's license. I was petrified.

The classes were held Thursday and Friday evenings, Saturday and Sunday all day, with Sunday late afternoon drivers test being the grand finale.

The evening classes were a piece of cake, all about rules and state regulations and questions that were simple to answer.

Then came Saturday, 8am, and on the bike for the first time, walking it back and forth across the paved parking lot fenced-in training area. I was simply overwhelmed by the feel of the bike, its heaviness, awkwardness and I felt like I was all arms and legs with no control over either.

By Saturday afternoon the class and I were slowly riding and shifting, back and forth, back and forth. The weather was cool but inside my jacket, I was sweating buckets and asking myself, why again am I doing this?

Sunday morning and back on the bike, riding around yellow cones in a figure-eight pattern, around and around, shifting, braking, and accelerating in unison with the guy ahead of me, then all of a sudden, my bike took off toward the high wire fence, I braked just before the fence imprinted itself in my face. I was shaking and sweating and dropped the bike.

Silence, utter silence until the instructor asked, what happened there? I didn't know. I was incredibly shaken up. The rest of the group, all guys, looked away and were respectful of my private time, I held the tears back but it was a struggle to do so.

These guys were kind in their silence.

I picked up the bike, got on, and began the figure-eight pattern again and again and again.

Later that Sunday afternoon I passed the test. I was so happy I cried! I did it.

MUSIC VS BUSINESS

WHICH IS HAPPIER

Ever see a sad drummer? Me neither.

For me watching a band play is like feeling every cell of my body sing and smile. The musicians strum, pound, blow and rattle their instruments in pure unadulterated happiness.

I want to compare a music experience to a business owner's experience and reflect on how often I saw or felt such joy in the company of fellow owners. A business lunch table talk can go like this; gee I am happy that my sales are down this month or wow the last employee is filing a worker's comp claim or how about my marketing person who quit and took the entire list of our contacts with her?

Do these comments warrant drum beat joy for you?

My guess is the drummer is not broadcasting his last week's blisters and callouses or backache and bad body posture, broken sticks, and losing next month's gigs.

I began to take notice of others at business meetings, especially when they talked about their business. I zeroed in on what was said and how the message was delivered. Somehow the fact that musicians radiate their feelings while they are performing and business owners speak freely about their professional business, seemed to me at least to have a connection.

I went back to a drummer I know, Jed, and asked him to talk about this. Jed loves the drums and has been playing for several years. As far as moving with the drums, he can't stop that because the drumbeat causes his body to move. Ok, I get that.

Comparing this beat thing to business then, I might say that the energy of business or from working with others in the business can cause a body to move in the rhythm of the business. Does this make sense? It does to me.

I discovered from personal experience and paying attention to what is happening around me that when I protect the good and honest and generous workings of my business my body and my mind show happiness. This happiness can be felt and kept to myself depending on where I am when I experience this joy or I show happiness outwardly during a staff meeting, one-on-one conversation, or at an event when the table talk is about owning, growing, and flourishing as a business owner.

This band vs business analogy works for me. When I first pondered it, I was in the audience of the band Jed plays in and he was drumming to his heart's content. I was amazed at his total absorption in what he was doing and at the same time his aura gave off sparks of being in the flow. I wanted that in my life so much so that I began to pay attention to what I was doing, why I was doing it, and how I felt while in the flow more intensely, focusing on my feelings and my speech and on what brings joy and happiness. My intentions changed.

My intention today is to have complete satisfaction in the work I do and the people I work with. This plays out for me like a band only with a different beat. When every cell in my body sings and smiles during business activities now I wonder if maybe I could learn to be a drummer.

MY INVISIBLE POWER

Lisa is my chiropractor, friend, confidante, and active mother of three. So, when I saw her return address on the envelope after my Mom passed, I was not surprised.

The surprise came when I opened the envelope and read the card. Lisa had reserved a Catholic Mass in March to celebrate my Mom's life.

That surprised me! I was happy, thankful, touched, and grateful.

Gratitude. Often expresses itself in several ways. It is more than a smile or a happy dance.

I believe Gratitude is honor and esteem. It shows up in a handshake, a touch, and a knowing deep within ourselves.

Lisa's heartfelt action was utterly thoughtful, and right on, I felt peace and love and Gratitude for our friendship and understanding of one another.

Gratitude is my invisible power. When I acknowledge Gratitude, it brings me to a peaceful place, powerful peace, I like to call it.

I do not think it is talked about enough, but Gratitude is often buried in our consciousness. I like to imagine it resting on the bottom of a vast lake. It is majestic, severe, and something to grab and hang on to. And if it was an animal, it would be an elephant.

I attended the Mom-Mass with Lisa on an early Wednesday morning. As it happened, this was a church event that included the elementary students. When Mom's name was mentioned from the podium, I caught my breath. To hear her name spoken again was magical.

And I felt Gratitude.

NGO WAS AN UNFAMILIAR TERM

I was in the dark with the term NGO until I met Susan. Susan is a spokesperson for a group of NGOs and has a number of personal connections. Because I was looking at disadvantaged women owned businesses and how I might help them grow their small businesses I was totally excited to meet anyone and everyone who might possibly lead me in that direction.

A mutual friend introduced us and I quickly set up a date to meet for lunch. I arrived at the restaurant with a yellow legal pad of questions and Susan came with a smile and gracious demeanor. There was so much to know and learn and listen and understand and I was totally in orbit!

The best though was at the close of our lunch Susan asked if I wanted to join her on the upcoming NGO trip to Uganda and Tanzania. WOW, did I! I said yes before I even thought more about it. FYI, NGO stands for Non-Governmental Organization. These amazing and helpful non-profit organizations are set up around the world in developing countries to assist thousands of people who live there, effective NGOs are located in poverty-stricken areas.

Landing in the country of Uganda was a mind-boggling experience that's for sure. The first morning as we were driving through the city, I was overcome with emotion so much so that I lost my voice. This did not matter much as words were certainly not enough to address the dizzying emotions of hurt, love, sadness, conflicted, surreal, energy, life force, crowded, hundreds of faces, humanity, and extremely thankful to be there.

During our time in Uganda and Tanzania we met and consulted with 6 local groups that received part of their funding from organizations in the US. These were women owned small businesses eager to learn keys and truths on managing their small local business. Lovely women, welcoming and happy, organized, and every one doing the work of business to support her kids. Admittedly this was a moment in time that changed me forever. We bonded, we talked, we shared, we laughed and we loved.

Fast forward to my return to the US and an unexpected health event that prohibited me from overseas travel for the foreseeable future. I was not too happy about the restriction since I had planned to work more closely with International NGO organizations.

I looked around with new eyes to find an opportunity where I could assist others who have not had the opportunities, I have of being born in the US.

And there it was; right in front of my self and it involved the business I already had in place. My business is a business of commercial cleaning, we work in professional and government buildings to keep their carpet looking good all the time. The technicians I hire are required to be self-starters and diligent, a lofty requirement for sure and to my dismay was not panning out with most of the people working, seriously I was looking for options to make a change. I discovered our technicians who migrated from Cuba fit exactly the culture and represented the business dynamics and values I had only before imagined. A fit between a farm girl and a Cuban new-to-America person.

What did I do? I was on the look out to hire more staff with connections within the Cuban community. I found that I could fulfill my obsessive desire to assist others who were not born in the US with the income and advantages I have when I employ Cuban technicians. A win for me, our customers and most importantly technicians.

Looking back to my renewed awareness of community and checking the backyard view I have a new appreciation for people who come into this amazing country to grow their future and the future of their family. I have learned a lot from working within the Cuban community, rich in culture and commitment, there again what I took as a disappointment by not being able to travel internationally transformed into the building of a business based on empowering others. Another way to demonstrate this in one word is: success.

NOT ALL KIDS' DREAMS ARE KIDS

Ever since I was a little girl, I have wanted to drive a big truck. I mean a BIG truck, like tow truck big or dump truck big.

My dad owned a business where he got to drive a big truck with a red cab. The considerable size was necessary as it was used to transport cattle and pigs. I drove it once when I was 20 years old, was able to keep it on the right side of a local country road, upshifted, downshifted, and shook in my boots. But wow!

Fast forward, and there have been a few times I have had to call a tow truck to transport a broken-down van. The happy part was that I jumped in with the driver for the ride to the auto repair shop. I talked nonstop, asking all kinds of questions. The high view from a tow truck cab is like, WOW.

Best guess is a tow truck driver OWNS the road. Other lesser vehicles move over, yield, and just stay out of the way. It's like King of the Road driving, and I dreamt for some of that.

I was not too happy this week when one of the business vans gave up the ghost, and now I am in the market for another work van. Especially when buying trucks and vans are not my ideas of good time management, more like a necessary evil.

Now, though, a regular medium size work van is not the best solution.

Since the most recent purchase was a commercial pressure washing business, I understood a large truck would be a better fit.

A large truck with a flatbed and large water tank, generator, and other equipment as needed in the commercial pressure washing business.

Initially, I was not crazy about adding another truck, but as I considered the actual need, it struck me that this was the dream I had as a kid, driving a big truck on the road, other drivers yielding, and me, sitting high like a King.

Call me crazy, but this is my idea of a good purchase, fulfilling a child's dream, which in this case happens to be mine.

You might ask, how often will I drive the thing once it is bought?

Uhhh, not sure.

NO HOSTAGES TAKEN

Lately while google-searching I found the latest HOW TO in cyber security to save all account numbers, logins, password folders in one easily accessible remote and secure place.

Is all the cloak and dagger security necessary? This is exhausting!

During lunch today, my husband and I were contemplating going "rogue" and buying a product business where we could not be held hostage by the "security folder". This was after I spent the morning online trying to add a staff credit card to my existing company account and he spent his morning working on why he was kicked off LinkedIn.

Yes, we were in desperate moods.

Hostages is what we are. Hostages to systems controlled by the internet.

Now, I ask myself, is there a business within driving distance, that I can manage without internet usability? One where "business as usual" is showing up in person or by phone.

Am I simply dreaming? Are these dreams reactionary and not probable? Maybe.

But, what if. What if there is a business where the major part is about connection and willing to experiment in what can be. Pretending

I am on the lookout for simple transactions that celebrate connections and require no hostage taking.

NOT ALWAYS FRIEND'S KIDS

Because I have lived in a few different places I have friends in other states and other parts of the world. Two friends especially come to mind, both have two children, and both I have had a close friendship of over 20 years. Felicity and JoLynn.

Today we are not close by living next door to one another but close in that we share a deep respect and love for one another. And yeah, it is warm and fuzzy when we have the opportunity to be physically together.

Every time we talk, the topics always and I mean every time, includes our kids.

Even though we do not see each other in the flesh often, in different states different countries, I find myself completely captivated by discovering and learning about what these young adults are doing. I love these kids.

One summer afternoon I was visiting JoLynn and while we were at the local coffee shop, I brought up a hassle one of my children was having and honestly, it was based on a bad or unfortunate or wrong decision made, (whatever you want to call it). JoLynn didn't bat an eye, and by her tone of voice and facial expression, I knew it didn't matter, no judgment. I remember at the time I was completely struck with the idea; she doesn't care!

I looked at JoLynn over my espresso cup and warm pastry and continued the kid-story ending with it doesn't matter does it, you love my kids no matter what decisions they make? Jo smiled and said, yes.

Felicity's girls are easy to love They are outgoing and lovely and personable and respect their mother. How can I go wrong there with feeling the love? These young women have their mother's laughter and sense of adventure, travel often, and not afraid to state their opinions on any and every topic imaginable. Our visits are priceless.

Soon after this coffee with JoLynn and spending time with Felicity, I began to take inventory of my feelings for my friend's kids and moved the feeling inventory to include kids I know, but do not have a close relationship with their parents. A few came to mind, then a few more.

I began a list.

This was a complicated puzzle and as I moved the pieces, I began to see what draws me to someone much younger than myself. And I was in for a powerful surprise when I realized the draw isn't the parents every time and in fact, the parents may just be a fortunate add-on.

The best way I can say this is that I surprisingly discovered it is the bold spirit, high energy, and warm character that draws me in, and when I am open to listen, learn and enjoy this person and all their idiosyncrasies and passionate views and language, I become more.

OFF CAME THE POLISH

It might be this if we agree that the last two years taught us anything in business.

Off came the polish!

No longer had we hidden behind our shiny shoes and career suits. We did not have to! It was exhilarating and freeing and almost worth the upheaval. Because today we are back to business, but not as before. We have more options.

The WSJ writes about staffing in offices and employees wanting to continue to work from home. What I have not read about is the sanding off, due to business disruption, of our polished exterior voices.

I believe we have become more human in recent years.

How? By showing up in front of zoom, phone calls, texts, and emails, we speak and write in our own language. Not sifting through business decorum or long lettered words, but friendly and looking to interaction as a conversation.

This has made us different and evolved into more human.

Going back to what was as far as business meetings, to show up and dress up and talk up no longer appeals. We have become transparent in linking our job with our true selves.

I, for one, am happily engaged in the 2022 new business protocol. And when I see or read an article that is stiff and formal, I feel less engaged with the author.

The polish is off, but the effectiveness and seriousness of business remain.

ONE PERSON WHO BELIEVES

I asked myself, who gets up so early to spend an hour or so sitting by herself in the cold winter mornings of Minnesota, to read and think before the chaos of the day begins? That would be me on hundreds of mornings.

During this "brain time," I often searched for ways to build an asset plan. But I found the reading and reflective thinking were not enough.

Something was missing. And I was determined to find what that something was.

Though, to be truthful, I learned much in my research reading. Books from authors such as Bob Proctor, Paulo Coelho, Kim Kiyosaki, Seth Godin, Norman Vincent Peale, Robert Schuller, and a few "how-to" on step-by-step asset building.

But it was on a week training program on real estate investments, I found what I was looking for. During one of the hour-long presentations, as I sat in the audience, I understood that knowing how to build an asset portfolio can be learned, but the disturbance of what happened next sealed the missing part.

A woman next to me had to leave ASAP. She received a call that her partner may be having a heart attack, and she needed to be on the first flight home. As she gathered her handbag, paper, and pen, she looked at me and said, "this is crazy; I know it is not a heart attack but just a way for me to have to leave this training." I was stunned. I felt so sorry for her. She left in a rush of sadness.

And then I got the missing piece. Support. One person who believes I could do it. Only one, or two or three, but one worked for me.

When that bright bulb went on, my world changed. I knew, I just knew that what I was working towards would happen, not only because I could follow the system of creating money, but because first and foremost, I had a person, a partner, who believed in me. Supported me and encouraged me.

I have a pretty substantial, I can do this myself attitude, but in reality, I benefit significantly from someone believing in me.

I recommend that we be transparent when speaking about dreams. And if no one comes forth to support, check out the nearest bookstore, and you will find an author or three who write with the purpose to help, encourage, and become a mentor/friend through their books.

OPINION IS WORTHY

When I lived in an apartment building with 8 apartments the couple that lived across the hall was white-haired, slow-moving, and quiet. I labeled them as very old. Neither one ever raised their voice, at least not that I heard, and they kept their door firmly closed.

Soon after I moved in my daughter was born and she and I had the opportunity to be home and around our apartment 24/7 and this is when I discovered that my white-haired neighbors had guests in every day at 10a, like clockwork, and many times again at 2p.

I was curious about who came and why and what I was missing and I had plenty of time on my hands. So, one day I knocked and was invited in. The apartment was warm and friendly and happy and light-filled and smelled like heaven!

Behind these closed doors breathed an apartment of interaction and acceptance and the sharing of knowledge and interests, this apartment was a home.

These two wrinkled and slow walking people held court every day with neighbors and friends, all about their age, and now they invited me in to partake of the conversation and offer my opinions on the topics being put out there and dissected around the room. Every idea and action were scrutinized and hashed over and the opinions were serious, thoughtful, off the cuff and many times hilarious.

But at first, I was hesitant to join in. I had this newborn baby in my arms and I wasn't all that confident in taking care of her not to mention starring in the center of attention every time I stepped into their home across the hall.

This elderly couple patiently took my hand and sat me down in a chair near the door, I could escape if need be. That in itself offered support at a time when

I felt small and uneducated and not sure of myself and my place in the world, and yet their actions invited me to give my opinion in the open and ongoing discussions. The brilliance is that without missing a beat or bringing attention to themselves they accomplished what they determined to do.

When I didn't feel like I could keep up with the experience and knowledge that collectively was sitting right there in front of me I punted. I spouted out ideas, my experiences, and opinions and sat still waiting for reactions, and boy I got them and was totally surprised. The reactions were thoughtful, respectful, and an expectation to learn more.

My opinions were just that, mine, many of which I didn't or hadn't or wanted to share with others before, suddenly I found a room of accomplished people who were interested and considerate of what I thought and said.

This changed my world. I began to look forward to the new ideas and experiences and who had the topic of the morning and how often we laughed and disagreed while drinking coffee and eating the morning's still-warm cookies.

I and my baby girl became a part of the group where it was a daily occurrence that I knocked on my gentle neighbor's door and walked in for the morning meetings, as I had come to think of them. My quiet neighbors were fakes, they weren't quiet behind closed doors, they were warm and friendly and entertaining and caring and open and honest and lovely.

They were my friends.

OUR BILLBOARD FACE

A few years ago, I had a friend, Jean, who had this eye-thing going on. We initially met at a Toastmasters meeting, and when it was her turn to talk, she had everyone turn to the person on the right and look into their eyes for 2 minutes.

She set a timer.

The first time, what a long 2 minutes! But we, in the club, were soon familiar with the exercise and even began to like it.
Jean has passed, but this legacy of eye-watching and eye-seeing a person remains with me.

I call it the billboard face, and the best part is that we all have it. It is our face, shining from a billboard for others to see.

Today, at lunch, I passed over the woman who waited on me, no eye-to-eye contact, what-so-ever, and I dismissed her without a thought. But now, I realize I blew the chance of making a connection with such a simple gesture as eye-to-eye contact.

Jean would not be happy.

I complicated this with rushing, checking texts, and mind hurriedness—me in a nutshell.

I aim to change. The first step is recognition, like today's lunch, and I am all in and prepared for the next opportunity to make an eye connection.

I understand what Jean was putting out there for me to master.

Faces and eyes are billboards to hearts.

Jean left me a red heart painting. No surprise there.

OUR FAMILY DANCE WAS THE POLKA

During my childhood and early adult life at every wedding and most Saturday nights, there was a Polka band or two playing at the nearby dance hall. We grew up polka-dancing across our living room carpet, learning the steps and hearing the music blaring out from the well-used record player. It was so fun and as kids we flew across the floor at a rapid pace.

As we got older, we hit the big times and were allowed to dance the polka steps at the dance hall. The hall was dark, had a wooden floor with a stage that dominated one side of the large expansive room, low watt lights on the walls and just a few in the ceiling, the tables and chairs were arranged in a circular pattern surrounding the floor, because you see the dance floor was the focus. And the smell? Beery, smoky, popcorny.

It wasn't long before we understood that the dance formation moved around the floor in counter clockwise flow, why? I haven't a clue but that's the way it was. And we saw who danced well and who to avoid dancing with and getting our feet stepped on.

So much laughter, sweat, music and community all at once. Many occasions after the last dance, we dropped by the local late-night diner for a plate of onion rings or French fries and washed it down with coke.

These Saturday nights were the highlight of the week and where we were able to see old friends, make new ones and keep up with the latest social news.

Polka life began to change for me as I got older, married, had a family and moved hours away from the dance hall and farm where I grew up. I missed it. New and different my life became.

My children do not polka dance, ever. They listen to my polka stories and marvel at how it functioned and how people planned their enjoyment around Saturday night dance halls. They make up stories and jokes about how it must have been, which makes me laugh right along with them.

Today I make new ways to do the polka dance, without moving my feet. Because it was so much more than the dance steps. Polka dance fulfills the human need of connection, conversation and fun and laughter and sweat and movement and not needing a gym membership.

Whenever I hear the music though, the beat, the accordion I am immediately transferred back to the dance hall of my childhood.
Lovely.

PANCAKES WITH PROFESSIONALS

Every few weeks, a friend who is also a young businesswoman and I meet for breakfast at a local favorite grub spot. I always order the buckwheat pancakes, and she gets a fancier kind.

So last week I was surprised when we met. First off, my friend plunked herself down on the wooden dining chair and varied her order. What? Something is seriously wrong, I gathered.

Wanting to get off on the right foot, I began our meal together by talking about a web show I was watching and enjoying the heck out of it. But unfortunately, my professional friend wanted no part of it. She wasn't having any creative ideas or encouraging news or show watching or good anything!

She had me dead to rights because, in the past, our mid-morning breakfasts together were filled with ideas and plans and possibilities.

This morning, it wasn't going so well, and I was puzzled.

Some background here is necessary. You see, this young woman has always been the life of the party; she doesn't have a bad day, ever. And now this?

As we talked, I asked a few pertinent questions, and she blurted out the truth. She hates her job, period.

She. Hates. Her. Job.

I sat stunned because this young person had never talked about the negatives of her job; it had always been more about other staff, vacation, benefits, and working from her home office.

So, what changed? We talked some more. As I understood her explanation, she is looking at the possibility of going back to the office workspace quite soon. She will be leaving her pets, working in her cubicle while older managers glance over their partitions to ensure her eyes are on the screen and she is working.

I called it out. This office environment has serious micro-management tendencies from managers who haven't figured out that many employees can work independently and get their jobs done on time, every time.

On the one hand, this is her dilemma. She is a qualified, well-compensated woman doing the work and getting to it every day, without fail, earning high marks on projects well done, still clocking in by the internet, and focusing on performance standards. But, on the other, she can't stomach the thought of spending her professional life in an office being visually monitored.

I hadn't a solution that morning, but what I did do was listen.. And as she spoke, she came up with possibilities. And that was precisely what this pancake breakfast was about, spending time with a friend, listening to problems, and after some minutes of back-and-forth ideas, waiting for one or a few solutions to show themselves. She came up with a few, and I am keeping my fingers crossed that one works out.

By the way, I didn't recommend the web flick.

POSITIVE SOCIAL TRIGGERS

WHAT ARE THEY

What a title. When I was asked to consider positive social triggers, I thought WHAT? In the year of virus/unrest/unemployment where do I come up with something that is positive and social and a story anyone cares about.

And then I met this person. Her name is Jill. Jill organizes a bunch of stuff but mostly is a professional at holding the apartment building where my mom lives at together. She figuratively and emotionally and socially and just all around keeps the lives of the apartment dwellers happy, healthy and satisfied.

So where do positive social triggers fit? During a time when I could not be with my mom face to face but only through the glass of a large multi pane window or on a zoom call I continually worried about her emotional wellness. And by the way what are positive social triggers? I dug a little into some research papers and found at a few triggers.

Compliments

Praise

Other Peoples Habits

Clustering

Authority

Consistency

Commitment

I guessed that positive social triggers cause desired and good change, the hint was in the word positive, anyway I began to pay attention to Jill's voice either from email or when I called her to ask a question. She was and still is today always willing to share her insights, which are consistently accurate, kind and generous. No whitewashing the truth but keeping in mind her responsibility to staff and the families of the apartment residents. This is where authority and consistency showed up in Jill's leadership style.

Jill's other tributes of positive social triggers I found out from my mom. Mom told me that Jill paid attention to her and other residents every day by either saying hi, how are you in the hall or would stop in to see mom in her apartment. This is no dark and dreary assisted living place where no one wants to visit, no these halls are intentionally bright and friendly, the massive fireplace burns hot and the smells from the dining room are delightful. It's a marvelous home address for more than a few people.

All this observation leads me to believe that a person can be a positive social trigger. I don't know how accurate that is but since meeting Jill and observing her undivided attention to the work she does, I believe she, her very humanness has been a huge positive social trigger this past year in the lives of her staff and the very people they serve in the assisted living apartments.

Back to the title: POSITIVE SOCIAL TRIGGERS what are they, I would surmise these triggers are actions, ways of being AND showing up in our daily work and life in a way that is supportive, nurturing and generous.

PROFESSIONAL PEOPLE ARE DULL

Listening to table talk next to me at a coffee shop I hear what are referred to as professional people and they are being defined in one word DULL. That got me thinking about who fits in their professional people category. Is it me???

After doing a bit of research I found that there are similar industries referred to as professional. At the top is finance, then corporate, then anyone with a fancy office. Well, that then includes me, my office is awesome! Another definition: whoever must wear a suit to work. I would argue in today's work-at-home status suits might not be required and then there are the jeans and white shirts, would they fit in as professional wear?

All this to say, I believe professional may be up to the speakers' definition. For purposes of this writing, I will define professional people as people who work in finance, insurance, corporate, and must wear a suit or high-end professional garments when working or meeting a client. And one more defining point, these professionals attend gatherings and eat breakfast, lunch or dinner served on linen table coverings.

Since we are not interacting in person all that often in our professional lives, surely not much hugging and shaking hands happening, I hit a snag when thinking of another opportunity to reach and meet and connect with more professionals. People I want to meet and would if we were at a networking function or awards dinner.

Taking a survey of my interactions I saw the way I like connecting is by reading honest words on a post, possibly on Instagram or in an email. The posts I receive that catch my eye are sunny and touching. Short stories that draw me into the message and the messenger.

The light bulb went on and I didn't see a DULL person in my sights. Since much of my past professional writing was about using popular words, buzz words that people thought were with it which reminds me of high school and who was in the in-group and who was not. I brushed all that aside and now strive to write emails and posts that are welcoming, honest, generous, and inviting.

As for Professional People being labeled DULL...nope, nada......

PUT ON THE SPLASH

I registered for a networking lunch event weeks ago and today is the on-my-calendar date. I feel like skipping it—no jeans or t-shirt lunch but dress slacks and ironed button-down shirt. Professional dress, in the fine print, is expected and acceptable attire.

That alone put a damper on the event for me. Did I want to ask the question; when in the balance of freedoms did women skip the part of jeans + jacket = professional dress?

Please put on The Splash, which is how I define professional dress. Because I wanted to expand business contacts outside of the current, comfortable and familiar, I did precisely that.

Walking into the community room, I felt a new vibe, saw new faces, and heard new conversations. I located a good seat near the back of the room to sit and absorb it all.

In the past, whenever I was the new person, someone from the organization usually introduced themselves, but today, not one member of the group did so. Hmmm. What to do?

I paid particular attention to finding out who ran the show and who was the person referenced most often in the first and last comments from the podium.

That person, I knew, was the connector and the best person to meet. So, I listened and observed, found her, and then walked up later to introduce myself and set up a future conversation.

This time The Splash worked out, and in 90 minutes, I met and found a new person to connect with and, who knows, possibly a new friend.

PUTTING BAND-AIDS ON SOCIAL CHANGE

I paid some money to support a group dedicated to social change. I understood this group's mission was to educate how we treat people different from ourselves.

I patted myself on the back and thought, "okay now, you are a good person by supporting this organization." And I believed that this would make a difference. So, I gave with no skin in the game and hoped people would understand that humans are equals and get over themselves about the "who is most valuable and intelligent" crap.

Later though, I believed that my giving action was like putting a band-aid on a massive head injury. Only not a colorful Superwoman band-aid, instead I applied a money band-aid to a society malfunction. Impossible to fix with so little foresight on my part.

But now I get it.

This non-profit organization was founded by people, joined by people, and run by people to educate the public in accepting others, everyone, all one, everybody, period. Okay, that sounds true and good.

But here is the catch. For real progress to be made out there, in public, leaders, volunteers, donation givers, and telemarketers of the organization must trust and understand one another. I did not know the interactions and relationships of the organization. Is there a trusting soul to the group?

I might be a little preachy but here goes; I believe that to create the society we dream about; equal, respectful, first, we must look in the mirror and talk to ourselves. Maybe the conversation would go something like this.

Where am I missing the point? She said it, but that makes me feel unsettled. It is new information. I want to be open but not look silly and don't know anything.

How can I accept this new viewpoint? Talking more will open the door to a sliver to trust. I want that.

I now believe that I was putting a money band-aid on a societal problem that takes personal attention on my part. Nevertheless, I think social change is critical for our country to be healthy. For change to happen, it begins with each of us Americans looking in the mirror, asking hard

questions about who we are, and building our relationships on trusting one another. Change starts with the person in the mirror first; count on it.

Do we trust ourselves to make changes?

Do we want to?

RAW PHYSICAL POWER VS MINDFULNESS

I read a New York Times article this morning about Russia and the move on Ukraine. And I was mortified by the way the writer talked about Russia's plan to begin the takeover IN THE NEXT FEW DAYS.

Not next month or next year, but in just a few short days, possibly 72 hours.

As I read the article, I saw that Russia expects to engage with pure physical military strength, such as bombs, guns, and planes, which means many people will die.

I have spent many hours in the last year watching podcasts reading articles and books about mindfulness and other people's stories. And I listened to understand political platforms from a different perspective, democrats, republicans, liberals, white, black, native, Hispanic, Asian.

Much of what I read, at first, I reared back and said no-way! Then I watched a podcast that spoke to me and brought me new ways of interpreting people. So okay, now I see that when I listen to another person's story and be open to what the person is saying, I may disagree, but I may also understand the why.

Like peanut butter and jelly, two people can be together, close even, but not thoroughly smeared on the same bread.

So back to the Putin decision of Russia and Ukraine. All the past year of studying mindfulness, other people's stories, and listening to ideologies vastly opposed to mine, this morning, as I read the article, I realized that none of my past mindfulness studies made sense in Russia/Ukraine.

Putin is stretching my ability to be open and inviting. I would be lying to say that he has a story I could listen to, which justifies the decision to invade Ukraine.

I came to this conclusion.

All the mindfulness and story listening in the universe will not change what Russia, China, and dictatorships plan to do. They speak the language of raw physical power and see countries focused on human rights as weak, decision less, and laughable.

Today, for the safety of our world, serious actions are necessary by leaders who can see the situation clearly and take action.

But not by me, with my mindfulness and vulnerability.

And that makes me feel weak.

REASSURED AND RELIEVED

My backstory is that I own a commercial cleaning business in Tampa, Florida. What that means is that my employees' clean carpets, upholstery, and fabric panels in buildings like banks, corporate headquarters, libraries, police offices, county offices, attorney firms, and call centers. We love dirty carpet and now during the flee from professional office to home office movement there is less dirty carpet and more time on our hands to think about where this cleaning business is going in the future.

The virus is the catalyst that caused a ton of change, that's for sure. We've asked ourselves what that means for our customers and for us. All of our employees are trained in the chemistry of cleaning products and are certified in carpet fiber and fiber reactions to cleaning products and systems.

What good is that in today's non-cleaning non-staffed office where hardly anyone is walking on the carpet?

We looked to the accounts that have staff remaining or arriving back soon. We actually miss interacting with the offices staffs in the buildings we service and want more than anything to see a return to that normalcy of our working social lives. We saw that these businesses have in-house call centers and many round-the-clock hours that are staffed, perhaps minimally, but still somebody or some bodies are there and a new service of providing virus and germ-free protection for more than a day or two to the touch-points is strongly recommended.

Touch-points such as doorknobs, counters, kitchen area, bathrooms, file cabinets, these surfaces might be horizontal or vertical but touch-points all the same.

I want to clarify touch-points a little further. Touch-points are surfaces that require surface protection with the application of a product that has passed EPA certification and intense due diligence by environmental services and legal staff, with every measure taken to provide protection and to mitigate the transfer of infections, diseases, and harmful germs.

We shifted direction and added employee hours to our training calendar so that we could provide this vital and, in many ways new and revolutionary, protection service. We were surprised that we were called the very next week to do our first application. Talk about perfect timing!

While this works for us, we find that office managers, property managers, and facility managers do not have the time or resources to use internal staff to apply this protection product correctly, nor do they want to for that matter, which is okay with us since we can step in and do this.

I could list an array of scientific facts and charts and go into details about each particular infectious disease mitigation protocol and new and promising nano-molecular, long-lasting antimicrobial surface protectants, but I won't... except for this one gem that I want to leave you with.

Once the right surface product is applied, please remember that the service then does not need to be scheduled weekly but can be moved to one treatment every 70-90 days, on average; a big win for cost and minimized office disruption.

Clarity so clear, a veil opened and life became all in all. Life, the gift of living and breathing, doing away with inconsequential problems and disagreements, focus now the space seemed to say, focus now and understand the gift of life and our connection to one another. Casey was the connection to everyone in that church, we were there because of his life and now during the service, I connected to something so incredibly beautiful I still find it difficult to put it into words.

This feeling of transparent clarity lasted for about 6 weeks after that day, 6 weeks of seeing my world differently and cherishing the simple truth I learned

from Casey, life is a gift to be lived. He showed me the way.

REGULAR THOUGHTS FALL AWAY

When were the times that what you saw caused a standing still of time and place and being? This was when every single familiar thought in your beautiful brain stopped, totally and completely!

What does your brain-stopped list look like?

I have a few remembrances that instantly pop: my first sight of the Pacific Ocean, the Mosaic Art in Rome, the people-packed streets of Kampala, and most recently, the black, craggy, and moss-covered lava fields in Iceland.

This is when, even today, you can see, smell, feel and be right back in that place, time, and season. Your brain literally stops the normal and allows for new information so incredible it stays within you years later. Is this making sense to you?

I recently found this physical reaction to something so incredibly personal and vital and out of my ordinary unique to understand. To notice and take stock in why this happens when it is unexpected.

Now, I have lots of stuff to keep my mind busy, jam-packed, and very focused on what's what. So, when this brain stop happened to me a few weeks ago, I paid attention. It gave me pause, and I found I wanted to understand more.

I dug into the experience and sought out answers. I discovered a new way to see what I had not seen in my daily routine.

I found that the more situations my brain freezes, becomes still, totally in the now/present, and because of this new experience and new sight, the more I expand as a human. Yes, this is true. After every one of the physical reactions of brain-stop, I come away with a new knowing, more profound sense of myself and the world I live in.

But these situations cannot be planned or orchestrated, they appear without notice until it just is. And then, the peace and joy and brilliance of the moment shine forever in my memory.

I yearn for more brain freeze situations, times when I see life more fully and completely.

REPLACING RESOLUTIONS WITH:

WHAT IF IN 2023

Like clockwork, I feel a disturbing stomach ache near the end of every January, and this familiar ache is caused by my list of unfollowed resolutions.

Drink less espresso-nope. Begin daily walking program-nope. Send more paper notes-nope.

Eat less sugar-nope. Call my siblings more often-nope. Build a list of new contacts-nope.

You understand I did not even START any of the resolutions I intently listed on January 1, and then, February arrives.

Sound familiar?

This December, I am making a different list. I have a plan for tremendous results during the 2023 year.

Instead of "resolutions," I am asking and listing "what if"?

What if: The business community asks for more service? Staff requests for more time off? The family decides to have a summer party? I discover a taste for sardines?

What if: is a sober tool for me. When I ask "what if," my creative juices kick in. The future appears hopeful and realistically possible. I fancy committed intentions with family, powerful business outcomes, and spectacular self-evolution. I want that in 2023.

When I ask "what if" the space surrounding me expands, new people share ideas, and my world of one evolves into a compassionate community.

Today, the black-bound notebook near me has the title "WHAT IF in 2023" in the margin. I have not yet made a detailed list, but it is percolating. And before January 1, 2023, I will have my "what ifs" list ready and on paper.

Will you?

SACRED ACTS

My sister hosted a sibling reunion at her home last week in Tennessee.

She celebrated us in her thoughtful sisterly way. We ate a breakfast of biscuits, gravy, eggs and fruit, rolls and slices of bread, coffee, and tea! And then corn, sausage, potatoes, watermelon, and pie with scoops of ice cream at dinner. Then, after all that delicious food, we waddled out of her front door. It was abundance to the max.

And we had a beautiful time.

Her family, our nieces, nephews, grand-nieces, and grand-nephews, arrived late in the day and made us feel pretty special. So many small bodies running around, certainly a remembrance of growing up years on the farm.

What stood out most for me was how she brought us together as a family unit. As we talked to one another, we discovered treasures that before were unknown. You did what? Where was I? Mom didn't know. Yes, I did that!

For a short time, we, us siblings, sat like birds on a wire, only now we sat on stools and responded to questions about our growing up years. Who got the pony at Christmas, raced snowmobiles, housed a zillion kids, visited a list of other countries, fell asleep while driving, was Mom's favorite lunch partner, or sued their spouse (that got lots of laughs). An abundance of memories.

It was magical.

For a short time, and on this day, we were building more, more family time, more happiness, more understanding, and more listening.

My sister has the gift of hospitality, which showed 24/7 as she planned and directed every minute of our short time together.

Today as I write this with soft reflection, I understand it as a sacred time of being and sacred acts of sharing, and I send my heartfelt thanks to my sister for making it possible.

Thank you.

SAY YES TO CHANGE

This week we are working through another business change that proves mandatory when faced with losing an account. And why? A lower competitive bid rained on our parade. What can I say?

Painful reality.

Especially now coming on the back of getting through COVID. We will work through it. Now more than ever, I appreciate our technicians and their ability to work flexible hours. They are champs!

What would you do when faced with yet another significant change? Buck up, that is for sure, and rearrange schedules. We are serious about emailing prospects and asking for their carpet, upholstery, and fabric panel cleaning. Why can't people walk on more carpet with dirty shoes, I ask?

Lately we are seeing a change in how we find accounts that would benefit from our personalized service. No one seems to pick up the phone, but emails, referrals, and keeping up a steady thought of making it happen hits the mark.

What I wish is more people in their offices sitting in their comfy chairs and asking if having their cubicle panels cleaned would add to office air quality. It will, and it does.

It is vitally important that we stay focused on what is suitable, sound, and doable during this time. Did I write that we are incredibly grateful for our regular accounts and super pumped about our health and the safety of our families?

We are proud of the work we do and have learned that change is inevitable, even when it is not expected.

And in a few months, saying yes to new opportunities will advance our business.

Saying yes makes all the difference.

SECRET AREAS OF SADNESS

Lately, in conversations up close and personal with friends and family, I noticed that we/people/everyone has a secret area of disappointment or sadness. At first, I thought this was something visited only on me but not anymore, sad is a familiar people thing.

I began to search out areas of sadness to find out the what, the why, and the how? What secret areas of sadness are we hiding? And I learned much more than I bargained for.

Simple answer: it depends.

Complicated answer: affects more than one person.

Instead of coming up with a questionnaire, I decided I would ask questions. Questions I made up as I learned more about the person I was speaking with. It was complicated though because we all have different degrees of life experience in sadness showing up.

Here is what I found.

Sadness can be beneath smiles, laughter, and jolliness.

Sadness is thoughtful and quiet.

Sadness comes and goes.

Sadness is a state of mind and affects our bodies.

Sadness doesn't play favorites.

Sadness hides and keeps secrets.

When my kids are not getting along, I am sad. When the business is losing revenue, I am sad. When the flight I am on is late, I am sad. This is not what I am speaking about.

The sadness I am directing my words from is a sadness that grabs us and makes it difficult to do our work, live the life we envision and keep the friendships that are important to us.

Now that is sadness, with a capital S. Deep, abiding sad.

Right now, a person I know is incredibly sad, his partner succumbed to a terrible illness. Another family member is incredibly sad, he is going through a loss of home and relationship.

This is gut-wrenching sad, the kind of sad that movies and books are written about and affect all of us.

I do not offer a fix or program or prescription. What I do offer is this: when sadness is shared, it becomes less sad. I am not saying it goes away, no, but may become handleable.

Less secret, less sad.

And when you are sad, that my friend, is progress.

SHAKY KNEES – DO IT ANYWAY

I accepted the invitation to speak at a business conference. The topic was one I loved, the business of investing.

I prepared the presenting material carefully with outlined diagrams on the plastic overhead sheets sent to me by the event organizer.

The attendees expected that the presenters would be experts and seasoned. Which I was, but seasoned or not, I was nervous.

What compelled me to do this was knowing the audience was profoundly interested and had paid big bucks to attend. Their reason was to gain information, and my purpose was to share as clearly and deeply as I knew.

If not for my purpose, I would have balked and paid specific attention to my mind telling me to bolt. And without my goal, I would have listened to my knees knocking.

A deeper purpose made all the difference.

As I stood and explained the material, shaking hands placing plastic overhead sheets on the projector, and heard my light-pitched voice, I felt my spine straighten.

My purpose was to share information, answer questions and be a link to other people's success. And I got on with it.

I felt thankful when I gave it my all and closed the talk. But the biggest surprise was the standing ovation the crowd erupted in as I finished.

The priority of purpose directs lives and calms shaky knees.

SHOW UP

I got the call. Severe sickness was a reality for one of our employees, and we were left with a huge void to cover in our staffing.

My job now was to make a decision. Do I hire another person and fill the position because no one knew how long recovery would be. Could maybe others cover and put in more hours? Or, I might hire someone to replace this person in a part-time position.

This I knew without a doubt. The service we provide must not be less than or downgraded. But, in the same thought, I was not letting this person go to find employment elsewhere once recovered. She was a loyal employee, and it is just not right to do this.

So, what to do?

The foundation of my leadership skills is recognizing the value of people. Therefore, when an HR event occurs, my guiding beacon is constant, what is the best course for the person and the company.

This time though, it was somewhat stickier. Because the ill person was a family member of others on staff. So......my decision would not only impact one person's position. It would, in fact, directly affect the attitude and feelings of other family staff members.

I brought the issue up with employees working directly with this woman, talked about hours, jobs, health, recovery, and came up with the solution.

I was pretty willing to pay overtime hours, and others were willing and happy to step up and fill the position until she returned.

Today she is back at work, and today I realize that we all showed up to make the best of a challenging life event. She, fellow workers, and myself.

SIGN OF MATURITY – NO BLAMING OTHERS.

I did it. I was wrong. Those five words were music to my ears not all that long ago.

I discovered my credit card statement had a higher balance than usual, which caused me a second and third look at the line items. I found what I initially thought were false charges.

Digging further and dialing back to the dates and stores, I realized that even though I did not make the charges, they were made by someone I knew.

This was when his maturity showed up. Not at first, mind you, but after some prodding and waiting and prodding some more. Maturity hurts sometimes.

Maturity: no blaming others, ownership of mistakes, wrongs, accidents, words, actions.

Indeed, this was a tiny event and not repeated, but even a small event like this stands out and speaks of courage and honesty. I could have forgotten about it and paid the balance.

What was critical for me at the time was the message understood if I left it go, there were a few others who knew, watched, and wondered about my reaction. So, a simple cc charge, done by one person, known by others, was an opportunity for maturity to show up, and I gave maturity that opportunity.

Fast forward. Every single cent charged on that credit card owed to me was paid back in monthly payments, and not a payment was late.

I am awed when a person takes on the responsibility of maturity and shows us, he cares.

THE BEST INTERVIEW QUESTION

Hiring is a catch-22, so darn many times. Even with all the filters and screenings and online tools available 24/7, we often get it wrong the first or second time.

What if there was a perfect interview question? It depends on the position, you say? Maybe, or does it?

Through research, which I define as input from friends, a courageous, insightful, and neglected, possibly minor general interview question is: what book are you reading?

And what if the interview took off from there? From the book read. There are automatic questions about genre, story, characters, actions, and author. Countless insightful questions arise from this one: what book are you reading?

And if you haven't a workable knowledge of the book, all the better. More questions and inquiries and details, the unknown confidence of a good hire is in the details.

Not only is the job seeker involved in the interview, but this person is also now offering description, interest, story development, and outlining the book with pleasure. A perfect way to build a comfort zone, create openness, and allow walls to crumble, and the safety of being ourselves is all that matters.

And what is your professional role during this time? You are the observer directing the interview with a razor focus on this person. What advantages and

benefits to hiring the right person the first time.

THE MONTH CASEY DIED

Casey is my nephew and was a student at the University when a freak accident happened and he died. A phone call and just like that the life and normal daily activities as I knew them changed forever. So many tears and heartache and mourning and yuck.

The world tilted for everyone who knew and loved Casey. My biggest wish during these hateful days was how could I take on the pain of my sister since her son, her love, her boy, no longer was there to give her hugs every time he left for the University. Pain so deep, our skin hurt.

We found ourselves in this mind state knowing we could not continue in such pain and survive it. But where was the way out and up and over the emotion too deep for words? As I lay in bed during those nights, I asked for a way to plod through the minutes and hours to sunlight again. "As night follows day and day follows night" these words rang and rang again and again in my mind.

Casey and his family attended a church nearby, the service was held there a few days later. His friends, family, and friends of the family were all in the building, the room was filled to capacity and overflowing as you would expect.

As I walked down that aisle and sat near the front I felt an immense weight of sorrow. In one accord the people up and down the rows were silent in their thoughts and respect for the family. Slowly, slowly change penetrated through the sadness cloud and as I sat, I felt the space settle and the raw grief morphed into blessed awe.

The awe of clarity, stillness, and presence.

THE SWING ESCAPE

As soon as the car stopped, I ran upstairs to change out of my church clothes, well-worn black shoes and my sister's hand-me-down blue-checkered dress into my favorite old clothes, summer shorts and red shirt and happily no shoes. Then I bolted down my lunch, cleared the table, washed the dishes, and flew out the front door as fast as I could.

I am in desperate need of quiet and peace and calm and no talking, just thinking and dreaming. This state of being was not simply found or easy to set up when I was growing up on a dairy farm with 10 siblings. The noise was constant and our chores were always top priority.

My parents valued cleanliness and chores for every one of their children, believing this was very close to Godliness and heaven.

But I found all the busyness of daily farm life constrictive. Not much time to curl up with a book and read which at this stage of my life was the entire collection of the Little House on the Prairie Series. So, when I found the wooden swing unoccupied and empty Sunday afternoons I then and there planned my escape from family. Let there be no mistake, I loved my family, but it was too much at times. Hence the swing escape.

Absolutely nothing beat seeing the blue sky with white fluffy clouds on a hot summer afternoon. This was living large as I watched the airplanes leave white scraggle trails as they soared across the sky. North, south, east or west, high and even higher just small airplane dots that encouraged me to dream of faraway places. I tried to grasp the truth that there were hundreds, thousands, millions of people that lived in the exact moment, at the exact same time as I, right now breathing, living, sleeping, working. What a thought! And this truth has amazed me even today. People everywhere alive and living the same moment as me!

My little legs kept pumping, the swing continued to rise higher and higher and my dreams of the future exploded out of me as I imagined myself traipsing across the sky.

The vastness, bigness and blueness created a hunger to know more, be more and love more. Here I found my magic place in a family of noisy kids, farm chores, garden chores, housework and school days. Swinging on the wooden seat is where I dreamt big dreams, lived large, traveled the world and when the swinging came to a stop my battery was recharged.

THE RED ROOFED OFFICE

Our office and warehouse were housed in an old tin-roofed block building for several years. It was white block with a red roof, old style beautiful and shadowed by the most amazing big and green and lovely tree.

We were content and happy and keeping on keeping on in the business.

Then I got a phone call. The person on the other end of the call wanted to know if I would sell the building. Whoa nellie, I said absolutely not! This was our business home. We had connected with so many people in this building, trainers, family, neighbors, strangers, delivery people, mail person and on and on.

But then I listened and listened some more. The offer, wow, the offer! Ok, I gave it a thought and more thoughts, then I sold the building.

So now the challenge came up, where to move the business? Should we stay and lease back in the comfortable and affordable building we knew, an easy decision with no moving involved. Or might we look for another location and purchase another building?

I took a vote, some wanted to move but Yordan was adamant that the business would not be the same if we moved. This was where he was hired and learned his job. I felt and understood his reluctance. This was where we had celebrations and food and music and fun. This was where we brought trainers in to teach and learn. This was where we ate together and connected.

I stood back and weighed it all and decided if I could find the perfect place, we would buy another building and create a happy place again. A place where

Yordan would see for himself that we can change locations but stay the same business.

I laid out the parameters on paper. Location and size and price and what I was willing to accept in a new location.

And guess what there it was!

Exactly the location I had dreamt of, the area between Howard and Armenia, off Columbus a block, close to employee homes and easy access to our cleaning accounts. Frank was excited and since he already worked with me as general manager, he now saw the potential of building supervisor, as in overseeing the construction and repairs of this "new to us" building.

This building wasn't move-in ready. In fact, there wasn't water access, the roof leaked, the back part needed to be attached to the front part and there was a small broken down, what looked like an old chicken coop, in the front yard. But I saw our future. We could do this remodel, maybe a better and more accurate word would be a major rebuild, anyway the papers were signed and we were on schedule to get the building up and move in ready within 3 months. Frank and I kept a tight rein on the timeline and he oversaw and hired and planned out every detail, I signed the checks and ok'd the plans.

A few important basics we worked from. The first being that every person who worked on the building had to have migrated from a Spanish speaking country and I wanted the roof red, the windows hurricane proof, the offices heated and AC installed and the yard rocked and fenced.

It all came together and every detail was included and completed within the time we allowed.

The place is beautiful! The roof is red. The walls are white block and the yard is fenced, landscaped and gated.

Which leaves us to Yordan's recent comment "this is great, it works out and is close to home".

TAPED EYE GLASSES

Last week I walked into a local coffee shop and ordered my regular coffee. The young girl behind the counter looked up sheepishly and said "don't mind my glasses, I haven't been able to have them fixed". Hey I hadn't noticed her black framed glasses taped up at the corner but now I did and saw the messy scotch-tape connecting the side to the front.

She looked down embarrassed, showed signs of distress and was over all self-conscious of how she looked with her taped up glasses. First, I felt sad for her then I felt connected and ready to change this poor self-image she had of herself.

Honestly, I didn't even know her name. It was the first time we spoke across the coffee counter and the first time I had seen her in this shop. There wasn't anyone near us maybe a few customers sitting by the large windows at the other end of the big room.

So, I told her this short story of days gone by. When I was a little girl in grade school scotch-taped glasses were normal. In fact, almost every kid who wore glasses ended up with them taped after the first few weeks of playing on the playground. It was almost a sign of passage that glasses had to be taped, and when the tape was foggy, sticky and messy looking, all the better.

She smiled. I didn't know for sure if she understood. So much younger than myself, a kid really herself, I wanted to be sure she caught the drift of "'when I was young" story. Obviously, there was a HUGE age difference between she and I. But no difference in the truth about wearing taped glasses that it is truly ok and maybe even somewhat hip.

When I walked in the next day she was at the counter and she smiled at me with her scotch-taped glasses! No sign of embarrassment, I knew she got it.

THE ALMOST HIRED EMPLOYEE

In the past, I was the one who hired technicians to clean the carpet when we needed another person to do the work. After the person was hired Frank picked up and did the training and introduced our new hire to the other guys already on board. As the business grew, I ran into a great problem that called for more trained technicians and I was setting up interviews regularly.

I began by creating an employee request outline and posted it on Craig's list, the first step was the online screening for the right person that would fit in with our current staff and enjoy being a part of a team. I found this system to work well for both the person looking for a position and the business.

Once someone passes the online interview, I moved to a phone call and if it seemed like a match for both the interviewee and the business, I then set up a face-to-face. Our office is so convenient and easily accessible that this was fail-proof when it came to getting together.

At this time my office was directly on the inside of the front door so when anyone walked in there, I was either on my computer or the phone at my desk.

One sunny, hot afternoon at 2p I had an appointment scheduled with a seemingly good prospect. Right on time, the guy walked in and we began the conversation about the job position. Expectations and job duties, personal interests and experience, working alone and with others, the normal interview drill. Thus far in the interview, I had checked off what worked and it seemed to be a fit until I asked the last question.

What about passing the security clearance at the county"? Any issues? Because you understand all of our technicians have a security clearance from the city and county, our accounts require it.

Immediate SILENCE, so heavy it settled in the room. And then a burst of sound, and from what I understood he had a felony charge that he denied vehemently because he was set up even though caught with stolen items from a recent robbery next to him in the truck bed. While denying responsibility he continued to become more aggressive until he was sitting on the edge of his chair leaning forward and I was behind my desk leaning back, he leaned more forward and I leaned more back until he was almost out of the chair and I was touching the wall behind my desk. Uppermost in my thinking, how do I get this person out of here? Not only was I alone with this guy in my office, but no one else was in the building until a little bit later in the afternoon. I then and there decided that when I got out of this mess that my manager, Frank, would do the hiring from now on. I gently agreed with the guy, then slowly and purposefully moved to close the interview while quietly standing and thanking him for his time.

Whew, he left after I assured him, I would call if the work came in that needed his expertise. But honestly, I was over and done and never again taking on the responsibility of hiring.

Once I confessed to this hiring debacle with Frank, he willingly and cheerfully took on the challenge.

The amusing part of this is that once Frank began to do all the hiring, we had happier people working for us!

Lesson learned: I can't do everything well.

THE BEAUTY IN BELONGING

I was 17 and working at the manufacturing plant of Tonka Toys when I first understood the energy of belonging. Tonka Toys is the toymaker that makes metal trucks and ships their trucks worldwide. Tonka Toys, non-union, running manufacturing 24/7 and hired anyone willing to work in the midst of the odors of burnt plastic, grease, and grit.

My job was to sit perched on a stool at a plastics press, guiding clear toy truck windshields into the correct box, checking for light scratches, and stuffing in tissue paper during the drop. Most important, though, was to stay awake during the night shift.

That first night I reported to work was scary. I did not know a person on the floor. Everyone was a stranger. When I stepped into the break room for my 30 minutes lunch at midnight, the small beige-painted room became immediately quiet. Being the new kid on the block was not too fun.

But after a few nights, I felt a change.

In part, the change may have been because I was so young, single, naïve, and smiley. I sort of always believed that everyone was my new friend. And I kept up the chatter anytime I had a chance. I am a *belonger* in that I like people.

I always liked the energy of a belonger. A belonger looks and sees others that can be pulled, pushed, or invited into a group already formed. At Tonka Toys, I was first the outsider for a few night shifts, and then I slowly worked myself into the group of press setters, operators, packers, and forklift drivers. At first, there were tentative questions and inquiries, as to where I lived, background, and school, but soon, people were walking past my press and saying a few words. I had so much fun working there, not the 12-hour night-shifts, but the people.

All my wages from Tonka Toys employment are long gone, and today I look back and see the idea of belonging and can call it out. Back then, I felt it but hadn't a label reference as such. Today though, there is more transparency, more deliberation, and more focus on what belonging is all about.

Maybe we have become a culture of labeling.

It is critical to understand belonging in our workplace as a leader and influencer. Therefore, we must create a belonging space, discuss what this means during our meetings, and include everyone in the discussions.

But duty or not, the simple way is not to prescribe labels.

Instead, let's call it out. Be human, act friendly, and make way for everyone.

THE BEAUTY OF AS-IS

I am referring to beauty as the best of now and being open to beauty as is instead of replacing it with a need to change.

There is the consistent question of "what change would be more effective or efficient" in business. And there are countless ways to be efficient, but today I am calling timeout!

A business has innumerable moving parts. Such as vehicle and equipment maintenance, account programs, and employee physical and mental health.

I feel the daily pressure to research new systems and discover employee empowerment ideas and find myself often on the treadmill of more. Regularly depending that I know what I am doing and our techniques are good.

Last week, the more treadmill became a problem, and by the time Friday arrived, I was tired. My mind was whirling at the pace of an out-of-control Ferris wheel.

What did I do then? I stopped, silenced my mind, and asked myself what felt so urgent?

As I relaxed and was quiet, I discovered this true definition of beauty. Right now, and in the moment.

Beauty knows all is well in relationships, commitments, and myself.

I found that as I acknowledged beauty, it was available and accessible. My job was to see and feel it.

THE DIME AT THE FAIR

Our county fare was scheduled every August, and if we were lucky, our dad would take us for an evening after farm chores were done.

I loved the barns, the merry-go-round music, carny voices, and the smell of mini-donuts.

One year, my dad gave me a dime to spend. So, I grasped it in my little girl's hand and went in search of a good carnival game to try my luck.

I am a saver, always have been. I like a few bucks in the bank. But, when I stop and remember my younger self, I see a young girl who did not like risk.

How then did I spend that dime years ago? After a walk around the fairgrounds, scoping out the competition, I stood up to the yellow duck tent and picked two yellow ducks out of the water. These ducks were unique as they each had a number on the underside. A prize to match the number.

The prizes? I cannot remember, but the excitement of holding on to the dime and not wanting to let go is forever in my memory.

I found that a tight-fisted approach would not always serve me well as a young adult. I lost out on an opportunity because of my risk-averse nature. So, what to do?

I needed new information to change, and the latest news did not belong to anyone in my circle. So, I expanded my circle to include books written by successful money people, signed up for a few classes on finance, attended seminars, and put myself out there asking questions.

This was so hard!

I remember waiting in line at an event; my palms were sweating, my knees were weak, and I sure hoped no one would talk to me. I just wanted to find my padded chair seat and gather the strength to stay until the end. Sometimes I walked out before the speaker left the stage; other times, I paused to listen to what the attendees around me had to say about the event.

I knew, though, that if I wanted to learn about money, I had to show up and pay attention to what was being said. Both on stage and in the audience.

And I bought books. From authors, I hadn't heard of before.

But what really cemented it for me? First, I had to follow the steps in what I learned. Action, move and cause something to happen without knowing the outcome.

Risk, little by little, baby step by baby step, I expanded from the saver to include the investor.

That little silver dime at the fair? A special memory.

THE EYE ROLL

When the doors opened, people poured in to celebrate the life of a woman. This woman gave with a whole heart, baked bread, birthed babies, weeded gardens, drove a tractor, wrote disciplinary letters to her children, walked with a walker, smiled with her whole face, and loved outrageously.

My Mother.

Mother's death brought us together on this day and time. This woman, she, the wheel, the rest of us, the spokes, all gathered to say goodbye and remember her as we knew and understood her. Each one had a story and came together to tell it and laugh and remember.

It was electric. A connection was made by voice, sight, sound, and touch.

We had three days to get it orchestrated. We referenced numerous pieces of paper Mom left with the details on who, how, and where the event should be held. Ingenious on her part, as we followed her wishes to a T. She got what she wished for, and we, for sure, we did. We got it done with the many details in getting the word out, check the church, how much food, who digs the earth for the grave, arrange transportation, whether it will rain, etc.

My family is not at all similar. Some like church, others, not so much, and then the boundless opposing ideologies about culture, lifestyle, parenting, education, where to live, how to live, who likes what, who does not, and will the Vikings ever win; a Superbowl! (I just threw that in).

Even without similarities, I felt a glorious people connection during the hours at the church and then especially at the gravesite. We connected. Maybe it was an eye roll, a handshake, a word, laughter, whatever. I felt the presence and energy, and spirit of the crowd around me. Maybe it was that we were in one thought, all standing around the gravesite and extending our gratitude to our mother, grand-mother, great-grandmother, great-great-grandmother, and friend by plucking a flower from the large bunch resting on the casket.

We loved her.

Mom connected us, and that day by the gravesite, I felt safe, loved, and embraced by everyone around me.

THANKS, MOM.

THE GENERALITIES WE MAKE

Walking down the street in an unfamiliar city, I found myself looking for the familiar. When that was not possible, I determined to see and observe the new and different instead of what my mind wanted to do, making assumptions and generalities.

I live with bias, tendency, leaning, preference, tilt, mindset, opinion, inclination to a wide variety of people, places, and things. Unfortunately, prejudice and generalities often go hand in hand.

Bias and generalities are undeniable. Yep and, it is a fact of life that we humans all have them. However, just because it is what we believe and how we process information, we are often correct in our assumptions, and then there are times when we are just plain wrong.

Just lately, I found myself making a snap decision without the correct information. There was this woman who had access to the hotel room registration when I checked in. I wanted to change rooms. I assumed, wrongly and with bias, that she was not willing to go through the effort to make the change. I concluded that she was too inexperienced and not trained in running this boutique hotel's front desk.

Two days later, I understood why she could not make the change. Two days of me misunderstanding her decision and keeping the bias of her in my head. That was plain wrong of me.

I was disgusted with myself and found that even though having a bias or opinion often helps with excellent and correct decision-making, it is when there is a snag that the tendency becomes problematic. A trap just like I experienced. I generalized behavior, and in that, I was wrong.

After I reprimanded myself for getting this wrong, I took note of what to do in the future. First, of course, I want to use educated bias when it is correct and convenient and the right thing with all my heart. But, on the other hand, I want to destroy any bias that leads me to wrong behavior and untrue generalizations.

Now I made a million-dollar promise to myself; I will listen with intensity and be open to changes in my beliefs and behavior while willing to make mistakes and be honest about those errors.

I will ask questions and look at other possibilities, and even do research. I will listen more than assuming, and I will do this regularly!

We might believe our simple biases do not matter, a simple wrong generality maybe, but I think they do.

THE LABEL OF BUSINESS PERSON

Every time I describe a person using a label, I want to slap myself. I believe labeling is an unfair and bogus habit. And when I heard a friend say, "oh, she is a business person," I was left with the question of "what does that mean" good or bad, happy or sad, honest or not, likable or disliked, approachable or rude, the list goes on.

As I pondered labeling, what became apparent was the voice tone. And I began asking myself, what tone of voice is that person speaking in? The tone of voice changes everything.

Many stated their major was political science when I worked with college students. As we talked, I found that some wished to be an attorney, and a few others had a strong interest in lobbyists. The tone of voice I used when I talked gave me away. My feelings towards law and government showed up in my voice. These kids picked it up and responded to the tone, most of the time with explanations and positive reasons why this major.

I had, at that time, concerns about successful futures in both law and government.

Without awareness, I showed up and showed who I was by word inflections. Then, on a good note, I noticed and began monitoring my word style and tone to a more open and welcoming one.

The end of that story, though, is that I changed. Awareness can do that.

So possibly, referring to someone with a label can be both good and bad. The gray area is in the tone.

Maybe.

THE OTHER WOMAN

I am "THE OTHER WOMAN" and it all began with the word diversity. I lean towards inclusion and using the voice of we, not they. For example: might we look at diversity another way, possibly leave bias and labels at the door and march in with honesty and truth-telling? Might we?

It all starts with me. I am the other woman who wants to shield her eyes from the meanness and attention-focused voices around me. I am the other woman who sees the diversity word as a means to bring division and hate to others, exactly the opposite of what I believe should be.

AND, it all starts with me. I am the other woman who sees labels as a means to divide and push and challenge and hate.

For 2 minutes let us think about this.

We are not a separate group of people. We are an idea. We are a belief. We are humans looking forward to a future. It doesn't matter what we look like as much as where we are heading and the incredible future out there for us as us, and us as the whole. Am I making any sense?

Let me tell you, my story.

THE OTHER WOMAN thing began when intolerance and labels and diversity buzz words appeared in every media platform and as luck would have it at around the time, I was asked to certify a business I owned as "WOMAN OWNED". Jumping through the hoops of producing documentation such as where the initial money came from, who hires employees, who manage the employees, who handle finances, bookwork, meetings, insurance requirements, labor, loans, vehicle purchase, office admin, buys supplies, talks to vendors finds accounts, manages accounts, sales questions, on and on and on. I filled out reams of paperwork to prove that I, own and manage and have the brain capacity to not run the business into the ground.

The hard part of this was that deep within myself I didn't see why I had to prove what I did to organizations that may or may not hire the service we offered to work with them.

I asked myself this question a zillion times, do I need a mental upgrade?

This is when I knew I was "THE OTHER WOMAN" deep inside myself.

And yet, I also knew to do the business and hire the people I dreamt about, the best way to accomplish it was by becoming a certified woman business owner and so I did.

Soon though, I realized that diversity or whatever label was hailed as the best buzz at the time might be merely a screen to hide behind. A word that brought up the hurt, anger, and terrible memories of past experience. These memories were many and real and hurtful with the bull's eye focus on women.

What was supposed to encourage, elevate and give opportunity seemed to me, did the opposite in many cases and was instead used as a media spiff and arrangement that brought out hurt, anger, hate, and needless competition.

I am the other woman, the woman who felt deep within herself during the certifying process and when awarded the certificate, that what I believe, truly believe is that all businesses are certified, all businesses have equal footing in bidding and all businesses have an opportunity.

I am the other woman, the woman who believes that labels hurt us. And I am also the woman who finds herself using labels indiscriminately and carelessly that hurt others and when doing so finds the door into the hate house.

The hate house implodes on itself once it is filled to capacity. It destroys from the inside out. It is filled with labels and titles and more labels and more titles.

I am the other woman who believes in a collective mental upgrade, why? Because I believe at our core, we are one and the same where it really counts, deep inside we want the same, the place where we believe love conquers hate.

AND, it all begins with me.

THE PERSON IN THE RED COAT

There is this person, a woman who lives a few blocks from me, in the house on a corner, the lot is overgrown with greenery and the white house stands tall and proud. This woman is a mystery woman who I have been wondering about for the past 15 years ever since I moved into the neighborhood. She lives singly alone not a pet in sight and not a jolly old woman who bakes cookies for the kids but serious and separate and prideful and content.

I saw her last week walking to the large blue mailbox just down the block, leaning on a hoe to keep her balance and slowly making her way forward. Walking in the near middle of the street, no bike paths here or walking paths for that matter, she looks determined by her stride to do her errand and return to her large two-story house on the corner. I am mesmerized by her determination and lack of weariness in her steps.

When I first moved into the neighborhood, I saw her in her yard and imagined we might be friends. I introduced myself and she asked if I was German, which I am in part, and I responded by yes, she said "good people" then and there I heard the heavy accent, must be German too I surmised. That was the first and last time we spoke to one another. Now it is just a quiet passing when we meet on the street near her house.

But I wonder at her strength and fortitude and overall keeping on keeping on with living. This woman fascinates me. Outwardly there are no signs of friendliness and no network of friends and visitors dropping by, her driveway is always empty, but she radiates wisdom, awareness, and been there, done that experience in life. I absorb into my heart as I see her actions are lessons for me in holding space for others, living strong and sure in decisions, and maintaining a livelihood that works for me.

This red-coated woman is no princess afraid to face daily life, in fact, I would guess she has seen and felt life deeply, it shows in her stance and prodding stride. Her face, her body language, and her question "are you German" tells one story. There is more though, more that I would love to investigate but that is for another day.

What a surprise and shock it would be if I discover this beautiful woman on Facebook or Instagram, would she then qualify for the last laugh? I believe so.

THE PLACE OF YES

I come from the place of yes. Yes, we can do that. Yes, that works for me. Yes, I will be there. Yes, we will make it work.

And lucky for me, the people I work with adapt to this mindset.

This yes place was our savior during the last couple of years. You can bet on a full-house that our forward-leaning mindset had a real workout when covid arrived. Then "what to do" became a constant rewind in daily decisions.

The business was dog-paddling already, and then our good accounts were frozen with inactivity. The push needed to look around and find another resource for us to make money.

We sat at the boardroom table and talked about what to do. Everyone joined in with ideas and experience and what's what. I was totally transparent with how the dollars were being spent. Always, leading with "staff gets paid first" as our company's strength and foundation.

We tossed service ideas back and forth and came up with a few that we believed would fit.

After the meeting, I began the search for the fit. First, I met with business brokers to ask what service accounts were out there, and I checked Craigslist and Buy Sell, and a few other sites where small business owners advertised their business.

I was on a mission, and the mission's timeline was yesterday.

We did it. We found what we were looking for and added another service by buying accounts and learning on the job. As a result, we changed work schedules, added equipment, focused on labor and material costs, and got through the worst of the worst pandemic.

We changed, the business changed, accounts changed, and today we are further ahead in our place of yes. We said yes to new business, yes to irregular hours, yes to wages, yes to out of comfort zone, yes to adding more.

Today we cannot return to once was, that is for sure, and would not want to.

THE QUESTION OF MONEY

I am a farmer's daughter, and since I was raised on a dairy farm where my mother worked sunrise to after sunset doing what farm mothers do, I gained a deep understanding of this phrase; "Women's work is in the house, garden, dairy barn, chicken barn, and pig barn." Mom worked wherever and whenever the need arose that called for an extra set of hands."
Which in my farm background was every day.

Mom didn't see a nickel of the cash earned by the farm. But, on the other hand, my father was good at finance and made money decisions.

This women's work idea bothered me when I was a little girl. And I believe because of that, today, I staunchly support women's earning power.

After my father passed, I asked Mom about their money arrangement while farming. Like, why didn't she exert her ideas more and question more? She laughed and said that this was the way it was done. It worked out mostly, and I discovered how money-smart my mom was from our conversation!

I have five sisters, and I do not know for sure if any one of them feels so crazy-strong about the question of money as I do. But, as women, we must ask the hard questions, dig deep into the stories we tell ourselves, look at our attitude around money and be financially independent.

Since financial independence is achieved in many ways, how I achieve it will be different from you. Money is a language (we cannot speak English in Cuba), and when we understand it and apply it, happiness, confidence, creativeness, and life is lived securely.

So, blah, blah, blah, how much can be said about this money/women in 2022? But, then, just when I think the topic is exhausted, I find another young woman believing that a partner, a husband, father, boyfriend, girlfriend, anyone, will support her, forever, as into the end of life.

Might her wish story come true? Sure. But my account works for me. It taught me that I wanted to be independent and understand the essence of money, enough so, if ever the need arose, I would and could and should support myself and our kids.

In the next couple of posts, I will tell a few stories about how my money questions were answered, in actions and mistakes and problems and happy endings.

The question of money has been an exciting journey to learn more.

THE RIGHT WORD

How often have you heard "what is that word again" from someone you know in the last few weeks? I have heard this, and the woman asking is frequently me. Yet, for the life of me, there are moments when the right word, the right tone, and the proper spelling seem an unreachable task.

I believe that what comes with brain drain is the right word drain. Word drain makes sense to me. When we are so busy thinking and doing and other people and making it all come together, our thoughts are tired.

Spell-check was a good tool for a season, along with a dictionary and now Grammarly. The tools are out there to assist in spelling, definition, and correct usage.

I might have easily sloughed it off, even when wrong terms or spelling appeared in my writings, until I began to get serious about who the reader was and what I wanted the reader to understand and learn from my posts. Only then did the words I post become highly significant, conveying my earnest intent.

I still get it wrong sometimes, the grammar correctness of it all.

And I confess, I make up words and use what I call background slang. Terms I grew up with, to mix it up a bit.

I encourage you to write down your thoughts. No need to post, but write to organize your world with words and expressions of yourself. Surprisingly, this is a way you can show up for yourself.

And I highly applaud you for continuing and keeping writing. Make it a life-long habit.

The tools are out there to use for correctness and understandability.

The bottom line to remember is this:

The right words are the words that work for you.

THE SECRET TO BEST ANSWERS

What is the best answer to a question?

The secret is not knowing everything; it is using what we know well.

Face it, we cannot know everything about everything, but we have life experience and knowledge of many things. So, the quest is to make what we know alive and personal to others, especially when asked.

Have you read Gladwell's "Talking to Strangers"? If you have, you will see many reasons why we do not understand one another. Facial expressions, culture, where we live, and why we live…. You get it. Lots of variables, BUT we have knowledge and experience, thoughts and feelings, and we have made good past decisions.

We are capable of good answers.

Answers are based on reasonable use of what we know.

Last Sunday, we had a Mac & Cheese Contest at our home. I knew our four kids and their families were friendly, interactive, creative, and fun. This I knew.

When planning, I asked myself, how can I set it up for Sunday afternoon to be memorable?

I planned with a focus on what I already knew about the kids. I wanted to use what I learned while planning and when everyone came to enjoy Mac & Cheese recipes.

We know more than we think about answering questions intelligently, adding remarks that stick and resonate with another person.

What do you know? What is the best use of what you know when asked? Think about these two questions.

Best use is essential, especially in the world we live in today.

In person, on social media, and in print, best use of what we know every time.

THE STORY, I TELL MYSELF

Story Told: We lost the account because we disagreed with our contact's viewpoint.

Fact: This contact was new and planned to change cleaning vendors no matter what.

Story Told: I thought everyone at the table understood the agreement.

Fact: Not all parts of the agreement had been previously shared with everyone.

Story Told: The woman sitting beside me in the airplane was obnoxious.

Fact: She was so excited to be flying from Montana's -21 degrees to Tampa's +70,

she could not hold back her happy voice.

When I got this last story wrong, I began to see my bad habit of seeing someone or something and coming up with their story, WITHOUT asking or finding out the truth.

Could I be more wrong, ashamed, unhappy?

Here I was jumping to conclusions without the facts and giving my brain a vacation from thinking. Pure laziness on my responsibility of living.

If I stop to consider, and instead of at first glance coming up with the story behind the person, place, or thing, I have to work harder and take more time, possibly ask another for details and descriptions and facts. This is hard work, especially when I am in a hurry or plain too lazy to make an effort.

The worst, though, is I find myself on automatic with storytelling. My difficulty is stopping to notice when I am doing this. Stopping and thinking, curious and open to accepting a different story than I imagined.

This takes bravery. Bravery looks for truth, differences, experiences, and wanting to make a definite change.

Next week, if you notice me moving slower, stop and ask questions more often; this is the new observant me, checking my imagined-made-up story against the real one.

I will never get it right all the time, I will continue to story-create even though I haven't a clue about the person, but I will get it right sometimes.

Count on it.

THEY ARE JUST PEOPLE

When we hear titles like President, CEO, Leader, Pastor, Speaker, Teacher, CFO, VP. We tend to

believe the human person behind the title is somehow different than us, and by accepting this falsehood, we treat them differently.

How wrong can we be?

Basic respect is always front and center, but isn't respect the same for everyone?

Just this past week, we held a training session at the company. I stood and watched our staff interacting with each other and the speaker, his wife, myself, and a significant account contact. Did staff treat anyone differently because of status? You know what I mean differently, as more respect, less value, or more critical.

I am thrilled to report that I did not see varying levels of importance or respect, no matter the title or relationship.

This respect has been a huge focus for me as a business owner in the commercial carpet cleaning industry. But, unfortunately, the cleaning industry, especially the technician's role, is not all that respected in "professional circles," and I have been adamant about changing that.

As we say in our training sessions, the change begins with us. It isn't effortless because we are from diverse backgrounds and cultures here at the office. But that is also a plus because we see our differences with one another each day. Talk about in our face right and center. The interaction causes us to pay attention to each other and what is happening on the job and plan changes.

Focusing is hard work. We pay attention to the small details of how we treat one another, checking our body language, voice tone, and facial expression.

One caution to remember is that we put halos on others, whether they wish it or not. With a halo perched on someone's head, we see that person as more worthy or greater than or more important or more successful or more respected or more powerful, and that MORE causes us to distance ourselves.

There is no MORE in respect or value, only SAME and EQUAL.

And the circle begins, us to others to us.

People (us), People (others), People (us).

TOO BUSY, NO TIME

Cliff jumping

I work in two states. Back and forth between offices and the people I work with. It could be an unmanageable life for some but for me, it works. I love the challenge of two different climates, building designs, and folks who grew up in a place I had only dreamt about as a child.

The back and forth from here to there has caused me to get quite specific about when, where, and what time I do business and see family and friends. I work well while focusing on a timeframe and usually can make things happen by including the main players in scheduling. Except when I hear TOO BUSY, NO TIME, that is a mind stopper. When I hear these four words I shut down and feel dismissed.

Granted we are a country of busyness and running around like crazies from morning to night or morning to during the night but when I hear too busy, no time, my thoughts immediately jump to posts this person recently made on social media. Huh. Wasn't that a restaurant, local ball game with friends out enjoying friendship, and hey, yes that is important, very much so, but please do not offend my sensibility by saying too busy, no time? Just be honest and say, sorry but I do not want to do that or meet there or meet with you.

More honesty, less cliff jumping. I may be the single one who wants to jump when hearing TOO BUSY, NO TIME, but maybe not. We could take a vote.

Busy and time are four-letter words that have become words with double standards. I find myself saying them at times and am appalled at myself. Marleen, will you just honest up and tell the truth, sorry, I have other plans then and would like to push this off until next week, month or year! Or, maybe never.

Okay, I may not be so brave to say next year, or never, but I am building up to more honesty in my responses and I want to invite other brave souls to be honest also. To make this work I first have to be gracious and accept responses that may be unlikeable but exactly what that response is, honest.

This takes maturity and I am still getting there.

TRADING ON A TITLE

Sometimes titles are necessary, but I believe in most circumstances they are not. When I say required, I refer to an occasion when it is essential to know "who is in charge" or "who has the required expertise" for the project/operation/joint effort.

I was waiting for entrance to an event at the airport when the guy next to me began a conversation. We talked about the airport and all the changes taking place. We talked about our jobs and where we lived. When the meeting room opened, and we found our seats. To my amazement, this guy was the guest of honor and received an award that morning. Not only was he an award winner at the morning meeting, but he also had a title to beat all titles. And he never mentioned it to me during our introduction.

After realizing it, I approached him and said, "I didn't know you were that person of notoriety!" He replied with a smile, "I am not all that important."

He certainly was not into title trading for higher regard or VIP treatment. I respect that.

I find myself forgetting titles most of the time once an introduction is over. Titles have been a pet peeve of mine forever. I do not care to be near anyone who trades on their title for white-glove treatment.

But people can get hurt feelings when I forget their title. I am not talking about the guy at the airport, that is for sure, but others who carry their title on their shirt sleeve for recognition. Indeed, it is their call.

So, the dilemma, how do I sincerely respect another's serious attention to their title and the title of others? Yet, in the same breath, I understand that titles can be hugely ego-driven, and the person on the other side of the title may require white-glove care.

Now, I know this is where sensitivity is required. So, I listen and look for clues and reactions when someone is introduced. Is there a wide-eyed smile as the title is said, a more significant physical reaction to title representation? There is always a tell, and it is up to me to get it right.

And I usually do want to get it right except when I don't.

For example, I was seated at a white-table-clothed luncheon event and noticed two men to my right. Both were speaking loudly, not caring or interacting with the others at the table.

And me, being me, got their attention and introduced myself. Neither seemed interested in me or anyone at the table, so I added some small talk and then asked about the large ring one of the guys was wearing. It was humongous.

Now I had their attention and unbelief that I did not know the ring, its significance, and who these guys were. They were stunned, speechless, and still did not share their names!

I was expected to know the significance of the ring.

The rest of us had a nice lunch while these two kept to themselves.

I gathered after I related this to friends that the ring was possibly representing football or other sport.

Not being a sports fan, I had no idea!

I see that titles can be more than letters or numbers.

TRAVEL TO FIND SECRETS

I love stepping onto a plane and landing in an unfamiliar country. I call the unknown a land of secrets because that is where I find them.

The wonder of land secrets was something I took for granted until lately when I was asked "why do you go there" by a few friends. I had thought everyone felt the magic of the secrets.

If you haven't a clue about what I am talking about, this is how it unfolds. First, a travel destination stands out during a conversation, reading a magazine article, or maybe commenting from a friend. Soon, I am on the internet searching for flights, transportation, highlights of the city, country, area, culture, and people.

I schedule and go.

I think this is tricky to write about but willing to explain and hope you get it.

Travel secrets are more than being at the right place at the right time. Secrets are waiting for me to see them. Almost like they are always there but never noticed.

Complicated? Not really, besides incredibly rewarding. Usually, I keep these secrets to myself, not sharing because it is a particular moment when I understand the magic of where I am, and I soak it in.

Today though, I will mention a couple because I want you to understand.

Iceland. I discovered a cemetery as I was walking through the streets of Reykjavik. As I walked the paths and read the markers, I was touched by the music of the birds nearby. Mature trees and vines grew, and some were strangely twisted, green on green, like a botanical garden. It was a moment in time when I felt deep contentment. A secret of being present, a whisper of love.

Ireland. Stepping into the Trinity Library, the smell and sight of long rows of ancient books was like walking into a bright light of wisdom. I realized this was a wisdom secret, and it captivated me and filled me with wonder.

Secrets are like a whisper without a voice. When I am in the moment, and a secret is there, it floods me with contentment, joy, beauty, wisdom, and magic.

We live in a world of secrets. The part we play is to notice and accept the gift they are.

TRUST PEOPLE

When it became apparent that I spent hours worrying about marketing programs, sales, vehicle repairs, accounting, the list was long, I decided to stop the rewind.

By looking back, I realized that business ownership felt exceedingly hard and heavy for several months, like an elephant on my body doing push-ups. I was not happy and did not like this dark heaviness. So, experiencing a weekend of worry, I decided to search out the source, where this feeling is originating and why.

I further decided to step aside for a week and scope out, adding lists to paper, what I did every day and where I was missing the point and making my life unhappy. As in, what was going on around me, and how was I responding to it. Immediately I felt the heaviness lift.

I began with what I knew had been my norm: working alongside my office staff in management. I loved it, and it is where I had always felt the most qualified. I listed all the calls, emails, and face-to-face activities for one week on the yellow legal pad.

And I recognized there was a reliable solution. I had to look and be open.

Slowly the truth showed itself. I had been doing more, taking on more, and worrying more about decisions that my staff was already handling. I was focusing my attention on their jobs! How crazy was that! Paying others and then taking on their responsibilities and commitments myself! A big no-no inefficient use of time and energy and boss/employee relationship. And I knew this! And yet, I took on what was not mine and, by doing so, giving me sleepless nights and headaches.

Quickly, I stopped the worry and focused on "what" were the responsibilities of staff and furthermore not mine. I went to far as to make a handwritten list so that I would not forget and shoved it in my handbag. A reminder that I hire qualified people to do the work, and because they can and do it, I can let go and trust.

This beneficial exercise is a Small Business Owners Achilles heel.

Trust the people we hire: indeed, not rocket science.

UNIFORMS HAVE A STORY TO TELL

All technicians who work with me wear blue shirts with white lettered company identification, company logoed caps, and tan pants.

It is their work uniform and worn every time on the job.

Security guards and customer contacts want to see our uniform at their site. It signifies that we are there, no matter who is in the uniform. The uniform tells the story of background checks, trained techs, and the excellent outcome of clean carpet.

We all wear a uniform. And the uniform we wear changes some from personal lifestyle to professional while always keeping the essence of the person.

Example: check out the uniforms of financial planners, bankers, baristas, plumbers, school teachers, university students. And then, think about the people you know: executives, car salespeople, and tattoo artists.

Sure, they appear in shirts, jackets, dress slacks when at the office, but even when they are at the beach, you might catch a glimpse of their uniforms. Tattoo people keep it colorful no matter where they are.

The point of this post is to recognize that we all wear a uniform. We dress for the position, what is expected, and then add our personal touch at work or home.

Me; I call my uniform "farm chic." At professional or personal events, you will find me in boots and, in most instances, jeans.

I do think it is essential to understand the uniform someone wears.

It is a shortcut in communication and learning a few details about another, no matter how small.

Do we care? I believe we do.

VACATION PAYS OFF FOR FRANCISCO

Francisco works full time with me. One day he asked if he could take his two-week vacation. Sure, I said just mark the dates down on the company calendar and speak with Frank our general manager about it. Francisco's family vacation plans were to take a couple of weeks and fly to Cuba to see family and friends.

Francisco is short in stature but big in personality. He likes bright colors and new cars. Always appears at the office in the latest fashion with rings on his fingers and a bounce in his step. He smiles often and shows me photos of his two boys whenever they have done something noteworthy and many time their antics make both of us laugh together.

But now Francisco is all worked up about this first vacation back to Cuba when he heard through the grapevine that some people get paid while they are on vacation, as if they were still at work. Never had this paid while seeing friends and swimming at the beach happened in Francisco's life before or for anyone else, he knew.

Francisco was on a roll here and he had a few questions that needed to be answered like how to see if this was true and how to check the rumor out? I was at the office a few weeks before Francisco's vacation dates taking inventory when Francisco stepped in front of me with this question: "do people get paid here when they are gone?" I said, what? As a follow-up, Francisco said I heard that people get paid here when they are gone. Ok, I was more than a little confused and asked what are you talking about, everyone gets paid here? But then I got it. Francisco had never had a job where vacation days were considered a paid benefit. My response was gentle and understanding as I replied with, we pay people when they are on vacation.

Francisco looked at me like I was an alien, he began talking really fast and said, you mean in my bank account? I said yes, regular weekly deposits will be made to your bank account just like if you came in every day to work like usual.

His face beamed happiness. His body shivered with joy. He had never had a job where he was paid while on vacation. And now he was in the big leagues of a steady, dependable job with the benefits that go with it.

This was some years ago and Francisco still works with me. What a pleasure.

WHEN THE SAME OLE ISN'T CUTTING IT

Raising a family and working in a business was my normal and daily life until it wasn't because now the kids were grown and the business was sold and suddenly, I found myself with more time and more thoughts and wanting only more of more. But I didn't know what more was. So, I began looking for more.

The mission was to find more and to do that I looked at a variety of lifestyles and money-making ideas. A mansion on the beach didn't appeal but finding a challenge to see what new avenues of wealth and personal growth I could learn and make happen did. With that in mind, I registered for a boot-camp that taught business principles with a heavy emphasis on investing annually held in Phoenix. I signed up before I chickened out. With the deposit sent in and credited out of my bank account, I was committed. It is amazing how motivating spending money on a week of training did to my psyche. I was too scared to back out at the last minute.

Never had I flown by myself before. Not only new to flying but when the plane landed, I had to get myself from the airport to the hotel, checked in, and ready for the early morning class. I was walking on eggshells and my stomach hurt. What's the worst that could happen I reminded myself and then I had nightmares.

Once I arrived at the hotel and my assigned room I settled in, laid out my stuff, and read over the itinerary, and had a few moments to wonder what a farm girl like me was doing in a strange city so far from home and everyone I loved.

But then I met Sue. Sue was sitting at the boot-camp entrance table and as I introduced myself, she checked off my name from her long paper list while giving directions on when, where, and what, doing 50 things at once but never dropping our conversation. She made eye contact with me; she was friendly and kind and I could tell she sensed my apprehension. So far so good, I walked into the conference room, found my seat, and got ready to learn more of the more I was looking for.

That was a tough week for me. Nightly I played positive and encouraging quotes and sayings from accomplished authors on my tape player, all through the night, if I woke up, I restarted the tapes. I was still scared but calmer as the week wore on and I met other students who were also stretching to learn new truths.

Sue anchored me, even though I doubt that she knew it. When I saw her in the back of the room or at meals or speaking with another student, I felt calmer. She was tactful in her questions and advice, never making me feel small but rather more confident in my understanding of the material being presented. I wanted to combine the knowledge of my past business experience with what I was learning new and take what I absorbed home with me to begin another chapter of my life.

I was so out of my comfort zone that a new zone had to be created. In this new zone, I battled to make sense of the new ideas and business education that was presented. Sue was there, encouraging and sharing some of herself during breaks and downtime. She didn't stop with her generosity after the event, we keep in contact and to this day I am thankful for Sue, an amazing resourceful gracious woman, one who mentored me and challenged me to be the best I could be.

I left Phoenix on a Monday afternoon after the event was over and found my way back to my home in Minnesota, fully capable of beginning my more.

WALKING IN MY DAD'S BOOTS

Working on the farm day in and day out, my dad always wore the same boots. Light reddish tan, worn near the toes and beat up everywhere else. Those boots took on the job of safety and comfort and most importantly were affordable. Talk about boots on the ground, Dad's boots hit the ground every day, even Sundays because farm chores were a 7 day-a-week happening. No holidays and no rest days.

I liked these boots even though they were rugged and hard to get on with all the laces, they were also sturdy and tough, like my dad. After Dad passed, whenever I saw boots that looked like his I would think back to my life with Dad. I kinda wanted a pair like his when I was in high school but nowhere could I find a store that sold tan, high tops with thick sole boots in women's sizes. Reasonableness would take over and I thought, really Marleen, you will look like your dad and do you want to look like that! He was bald and wore bib overalls.

But the color, shape and style of the boots were always there in my head. So, one day years after my dad passed away, I was walking down main street and pasted a boot shop and guess what? My dad's boots were sitting right there on a wooden shelf in the store window. I waltzed in and asked if they were by chance now sold in women sizes and they were! Oh, happy day! I absolutely had to have a pair. I sat in the chair and tried on the boots. Oh my god, they fit! Without asking the price I bought the boots and wore them out of the small boot shop. They felt good, springy and fun. I was so happy and excited and thrilled to finally have these farm boots on my feet, I took a photo and posted to Facebook.

After my initial joy I came back to earth and wondered what professional woman wears farm high top tan boots with a thick sole? Anyone? UGH. Ok, I planned to try out this boot style at the local coffee shop. The shop was considered upscale and there were an eclectic group of regulars who daily stopped for coffee. I put on the boots and hesitantly walked in and stood at the counter in full view of everyone and then……a guy walked up behind me and said "like your boots". Done. I was sold on the look and on acceptance.

WHAT COLOR ARE YOUR NAILS

I have a frequent appointment at a nail salon where all the nail techs speak a foreign language and our version of English is not their first language. Small gestures and voice tone and humor are over my head in understanding. These techs are consistently happy so much so that I look forward to my appointments and haven't ever been disappointed.

Now consider the job of every tech, cleaning, polishing, clipping, applying color, and buffing out nails on hands and feet. I schedule my appointments with Kim, who has worked at this salon for several years. While Kim sits across the small lamp lighted table buffing my fingernails, do I see her as valuable, educated, mature, honor worthy?

I think about these things.

When I cannot understand the language and chatter back and forth and my questions are lost in translation it is at times easier not to talk. Or maybe if I speak a bit louder my question will be understood? Reminds me of the habit of speaking louder to someone who is elderly or blind or different in some way and that by raising my voice, that person will better understand what I am saying, ludicrous and foolish.

Early on I realized the cost of having nails done at this salon is not the same as charged at other salons but yet the service is impeccable and polite and satisfactory. Right away I decided to add a tip after each service that aligns with what other salons charge. It is only right.

Not too long ago I was at the salon during lunchtime and heard a lot of noisy activity coming from the back room, it turns out these resourceful nail techs were cooking a bunch of sweet corn. When I was ready to leave a young woman brought out a beautiful cob of yellow corn for me to enjoy. I was overwhelmed with the kindness and happiness and politeness of Kim and the others. Laughingly I drove away from the salon with a cob of corn in one hand and the other on the steering wheel.

Made my day.

WHAT COLOR IS SMALL BUSINESS

Lately, I have been asking small business owners this question: if your small business was a color, what would it be? I got a rainbow of responses and colors.

We see houses, vehicles, grass, oceans, highways, and flowers in color and that color lends to our happiness. What about business? Might a business change its colors?

A master plumber sees his small business in green, whereas for the high-end property manager, it is blue, then the gentleman who lists and sells small businesses replied with soft pink. And there is me, and I see my business in cool distinct red. So, digging further to understand, I asked why blue, green, or pink? Are you happy?

These successful people say they are happy. Blue, green or pink are not happy business colors for me, but I was there in person, and I would say they sure looked happy!

As for myself, I see red as powerful, strong, yet mindful of people and the environment. On the other hand, pink seems weak to me, but not for the guy who chose it to describe his business, He needs a little momentum to take off, not vulnerable but in the foundation stage, he declared.

Blue and green, settled and steady. Both business owners have been in their respective businesses for many years. They are looking forward to the next 5-7 years when they will no longer be the person in charge of the daily work; I guess that makes sense. They both like what the business has brought them, financial security, relationships, and lifestyle. And they were most definite about being happy.

I wondered why those colors do not work for me. Why not purple or orange or black, for that matter? Indeed, there is a profound psychological reason, and the simple is that I relate differently.

Here though, is why I asked the question in the first place. I wanted to shake up ideas about business ownership. And I wanted us to think about our feelings concerning our businesses. Not an exercise you might find at "Executive Management Boot Camp" nonetheless, an excellent way to assess, grade, and appraise a person's relationship with business and their success.

I have had this on my mind for a while. The colors of business lead to when and why my color red would become redder or change totally to, let's say, purple?

Because you see, I had forever viewed my business as red, even when it was just a fledgling and I was trying to hire every Tom, Dick, or Harry, the red never changed.

Speaking with business owners about color was a fun exercise. First, the owners I asked were struck silent at the question, then they smiled and had multiple justifications to "what color is your small business."

WHAT DO I HAVE TO OFFER

Working, working, always working at the dailies. Dailies as in checking email, responding and deleting, moving information back and forth. Office time in and office time out.

Enjoying the job and position of small business owner.

One day, out of the blue, I was asked by a business acquaintance if I would sit in on a small business panel at a monthly entrepreneurs meeting that was held at the University. I asked for the agenda and found that I was not only expected to sit and listen but to bring to the discussion knowledge and proven success strategies I had successfully implemented in my business.

My immediate and spontaneous reaction was this: what was I expected to bring to the discussion as I was just a small business owner, promoting and managing a business, keeping up with things that business owner's do, not paying much attention to distractions, always juggling the bouncing balls to keep up with the dailies.

I hesitantly said sure, I can be there, and since the date was weeks away, I put it out of my mind. How time flies, and before I felt that I was prepared and ready I am sitting at the panel table, staring at the number of people in the audience and asking myself, how did I think this was a good decision? What do I, a small-time business owner have to add to all the knowledge and experience of the adults in the room? In over my head yet again.

Being in over my head was familiar territory to me as I jumped in with both feet to own my small business, and then proceeded to hire, fire, and organize it to reflect the culture and attitude I deemed important as a successful business, then took a few trips to support small women-owned businesses in countries other than the US, then found the perfect building to house the business and bought it! So, I guess I did have some experience to talk about.

As the questions began, the panel people who sat beside me referred to me more and more throughout the discussion, until I finally realized that I WAS THE ONLY ACTUAL person on the panel who was an owner, yikes, the pressure was on. I kept answering the many questions asked, usually relating my experience and the lessons I came away with and enjoying the interaction of panel and audience. What a grand time!

Before I realized it, the event was ending, the time had flown by. As I walked out, I looked back at the panel table and rows of attendee chairs and was thankful I had said yes, weeks before.

Is there anything more satisfying than an evening talking with other professionals about similar interests, opportunities, and experiences? What we have to offer isn't always what we see, but maybe about what we learn when we listen to one another.

WHAT IF NOTHING CHANGES

I read fiction and non-fiction, listen on zoom calls, participate in local membership groups, love TED Talks and even ask for help by sending emails.

What if nothing changes? What if all this learning, education, and asking leads to the same 'ole same ole' outcomes?

I am talking about outcomes such as regular business and personal concerns: no change, no deviation, or growth.

But that is just it. I might not see change or growth, or goals coming together, but that does not mean it is not right in front of me.

This morning, I was on a training sales call. My role was to listen and look for anything new and creative, something different, spell-binding, or a fantastic idea. This call was 60 minutes, and participant interaction was encouraged. I messaged a few times during the presentation.

And I discovered that I do know more than I thought I did. The presentation was terrific, the presenters knew their stuff, and since the focus was on sales in my industry, I felt wise when they shared what works.

From experience, learning, reading, listening, and asking, I viewed the developments in myself in a new way during this call. And it proved that even when shifts are invisible to oneself, they show up at the right time, and the timing is perfect.

I wrote down a few points about the person buying the service—commitment, returning calls, and wordage that is important in understanding the process. And then I took a breath and smiled, knowing the industry was in good hands with these two men leading the pact.

WHAT IMAGINATION?

My imagination highlights what I am capable of and how others react. For example, I imagine my Wednesday appointment will lead to a new account. My son, John, will remember the upcoming birthday, or next month I suspect that new prospect will commit, or next year will be the year that leads to world harmony. You get it. Imagination can be fun, playful but also be a wishing that directs and guides.

Fifteen years ago, I imagined a regional business with high revenue and many customers and many employees, and the talk of the state. Today, we continue in our cleaning business and last month added another service. We are thriving at a slow rate and are happy to say so. We clean carpet in government buildings, corporate headquarters, and professional offices and are confident in our long-term relationships.

We added the service of power pressure washing, which means that now parking areas and sidewalks are being cleaned and the gum scraped by our employees.

I look back and read the notes of that 15 year ago imagined future (and who wouldn't) of largeness in money, staffing, and recognition and compare it to today's reality. And surprise! The supposed large business numbers are not there. Which leads to the serious question of what changed?

I want to say the economy, which would be true and a way to pass off honesty and transparency.

The actual answer, though: I changed, as the leader and owner of the business, the choices I made and decisions carried out made all the difference. What I imagined 15 years prior, I no longer identify as a success story. The large company with many employees and media recognition no longer appealed.

Here is what I did. I substituted significant business goals with goals of productive and value-driven relationships. These goals made more sense to me and aligned with my "why." I was shooting for values and working with pleasant people who seemed as important as money or the largeness I imagined 15 years prior.

You ask what about the next 15 years? For the next 15 years, happy employees and honest relationships with every customer. Business success, as I imagine.

WHAT'S NEXT

It's not what you've done; what you do next defines you.

I am at a place in my life where I am making a professional change. So, when I read the above phrase, I stopped and mulled it over.

Does this mean every good deed done in the past is no longer necessary? Important maybe, but not defining? Or an act possibly defined me in the past, but no longer is it relevant at that moment in time.

And by define, I mean by definition; a deed that describes or characterizes or explains or represents me, my thoughts, values, and morals.

Simply put, a deed that allowed me to be transparent, see-through, known, and vulnerable.

Yes, I have decided that I really do like that phrase. No longer is something done in the past relevant. It has a timeline attached and cannot be sustained forever and ever. Because if it was, why bother with my next and the next after that.

Ok, so I buy into this phrase in that context, but what about future deeds.

As I research my next projects and position, I keep looking for the right fit. For example, I had a purchase agreement on a small business; I discovered a few concerns on the last day of due diligence, and I backed out of the deal. Not like me, but I felt a catch and listened to it at the last minute.

If you, the reader, and I have agreed that what we do next defines us, I want to be unconquerably sure the deeds I do next align with me.

And why is this so important to me today? I view the next ten years as the last go-around before I step away from professional life, and I want every deed I do from now until then to prove the phrase:

It's not what you've done; what you do next defines you.

WHAT DOMAIN TRANSFER?

At the beginning of the month, I closed on a pressure washing business. This purchase was considered every which way and finally, I decided that pressure washing would be a good service to add as a new business and as an added service for our existing accounts.

Immediately after the signing of the papers, the seller and I sat down to fill out the required documentation to transfer the website domain to my account. We filled, signed, emailed, and called to follow up to be sure that every t was crossed and I dotted.

After one week, there was no activity of the transfer in the new domain account. Soon my calls and on-line chats began in earnest and I continued to receive responses that said the transfer will take place in the next 24-48 hours, the first time I believed it but then it was repeated so often that it became several 24-48 hours ago.

I contacted the seller, Jim, who contacted the domain vendor to be sure all information was correct and in line for the transfer, like me, his phone call outcome was to wait 24-48 hours and it will appear in the new account.

The end of the month came and I braced myself for another phone call since the last time I checked the account, the domain in question had not been there.

I also knew that I wanted this resolved ASAP with guarantees. So, I punched in the 800 number and waited for someone to pick up. 20 minutes.

Finally, a hello and a voice spoke and I stated the issue and waited while he put me on hold to do the research. The system was slow he said and we waited, so long that when I didn't hear his breathing or the background noise, I asked are you still there? Yes, he was.

During the minutes when he was not talking and we were both waiting I found myself speaking to myself with words something like this. I do not want to be a screaming maniac; this is not how I treat others or what I value. I am so frustrated.

When I wanted to reach through the phone and grab this guy, I began writing my feelings and reactions on the closest piece of white paper I found. I couldn't change the long-drawn-out wait time but I could change myself and my reaction.

The phone call went on for about 45 minutes, 45 x 60 seconds = 2700 seconds during which I sat essentially in the black hole of waiting and discouragement. All the while I reminded myself again and again that I choose to not respond in a way that embarrasses both the technician and myself. What I will do is stay true to myself and when the technician is finished, I will end the call on a civil note. Which I did.

As far as the domain transfer? Let's wait 24-48 hours and see.

WHAT'S GOOD ABOUT THREE L'S

Last week my son asked me, "how do you talk to one of us kids if you see something not going well in our marriage"?

Good Question.

At first, I was tongue-tied. A zillion thoughts roared into my mind about sensitivity, experience, differences, ages, and Mom-Acceptance. But I did have a few answers in the spur of that moment. Since that call, I have given this question much more thought. And I discovered most of my question/answer specifics not only pertain to the seriousness around marriage but are based on a foundational belief.

The belief of the Three L's.

Love

Listen

Learn

Here is a short version of how this works for me.

First, and above all else, who is asking? Do I or can I love the asked? If not, why not?

Start there. With the openness of love, in this case, interpreting love as respect and acceptance, I freely hear what is being asked.

Then, listen. Love opens up the mind, and listening opens up our hearing. We hear with body posture, ears, and facial expression.

The last of the Three L's is learn. Once we open by love and listen to what is said, we learn from the teller. The person telling the story or situation, we learn what they mean, how they feel, and why they are speaking about this.

And only then can the goodness of understanding and change occur.

I have experienced this in business too. Managers utilize the Three Ls of Love, Listen and Learn, and soon these same managers receive the highest reviews from fellow staff. Proof positive.

There is much goodness to be seen in the Three Ls. It is easy to remember, Love, Listen, and Learn.

WHEN A BOOK COMES ALIVE

Yesterday I finished reading a book that spoke to my heart. The story was based on true facts about life in America in the 1930's and 1940's the era when my parents became adults.

We are talking about tough years for millions of Americans. The drought, no money, no jobs, families separated and fear ruled the country. I found myself captivated by the book.

I identified with one of the characters and felt a kinship and connection, a mother bond. Not so different here from there. I was pulled in by the strong and steady actions of the characters in the book. What was crystal clear was the deep drive of the parent daily challenges such as finding food, sickness without a doctor near, and moving from town to town without a car, on foot without shoes. It was the values these people lived by that inspired and pushed me to keep reading.

Let's focus on one example: in the book diligent field workers were paid little per hour and then the large land owner decided to pay even more little per hour to keep the workers fearful of losing their jobs. Or another example where certain people were only allowed in the hospital and schools while others deemed unworthy to enter. This is a bunch of crap! It made me angry. My childhood was spent on a farm we picked rocks out of fields, pulled weeds out of long rows of green vegetables and kept the animals fed, field work is hardly foreign to me and boy is it back breaking work!

My family and the community I live in does not do field work but this doesn't mean we do not have similar issues.

Have we not learned from history?

This is personal not only for me but the person living down the street or working in the next state or living in the north woods. I became infuriated while reading about the plight of others and spent many minutes thinking about life in the 1930's and 1940's. I spoke with my mom about these years. She remembers the dust and dirt the hot and dry and living on the farm with her grandparents. Luckily for them, they held on and came through these tough years and were able to continue their farm life.

Reading these 300+ pages changed me – this simple story with not so simple meaning and serious historical truths caused me to sit up and pay attention to what I believe and what I do because more than anything else I know that my actions speak.

Today I look around my place on this earth and see good people with good intentions and good actions and I have hope.

WHAT DOES FAILURE LOOK LIKE

Different looks for different folks. I suggest that failure evolves and that it depends. This month it might mean 5 extra pounds, next month too many work hours, and then again forgetting to put out the trash.
Failure working definition: a problematic state of being. Not actions but the way we look at results.

I want to shine a spotlight on this word since it causes great angst. My daughter persistently reminds me that I am too optimistic. She believes positivity is an unwillingness to face the truth. On the other hand, I remind her that seeing life and actions from a happy place is emotionally rewarding. We are both right.

This post is not about changing minds to think positive thoughts. Instead, it is about addressing the issue of failure as a state of mind and that our actions, when followed by evaluation, continue to come up short every darn time.

This is what I do when failure shows up and creeps in. I punt. I decide, yup, that failed, and I use the word failed, not afraid of it, face the outcome, and then feel the disappointment or anger for a bit, then I shake myself and get the feeling off and move on. Easy, nope. Helpful, yes.

Sound simple? Sure. Is it? Not always. But gets less challenging every time.

And yes, my daughter is half right. I tend to see life from positivity, which helps me get a step up on this. But, on the other hand, she leans to the negative, and that lean gives her an advantage in creative problem-solving.

So, it seems we are both right.

What matters most is that a failure mindset is accepted and then moved out of the way.

I keep working on this.

WHEN RED MEANS GO

I am in the midst of a Life Lesson in moving forward to achieve goals.

One minute I figure out that the best possible forward movement is GREEN – GO, make the purchase, and then RED- STOP sneaks up.

The opportunity before me fits the lifestyle and life choices I admire in many ways. On the outside, it is perfect. And with a few years of commitment, the buying decision might even be spectacular!

Be the RED is causing some trepidation and hesitation. And a few "what ifs" that keep me up at night.

What I know is that I want this in my life. I want to grow past who I am today, add more choices to the people I work with, and expand my reach.

I rack my brain, asking why I feel a RED when I know GREEN is what matters most. The little secret I recognize is that making this buy decision will test me and cause activity where I must expand past my perfectly contented comfort zone.

Ah, scary.

The decision is alive, front and center in my thoughts, so much so that I wake up with a big RED, as in a flashing stop sign. I guess you could say this choice is running rampant in my brain.

There has been a lot of assessment and calculation, writing lists, speaking with others, and answering doubts.

GREEN is smiling a go-ahead.

Today I decided to make pesty RED into GREEN. I signed the purchase and am excitedly looking ahead to what might be.

RED became GREEN, and so happy it did.

WHEN TIME-OUT CALLS MY NAME

After a long time of working, mothering and wife-Ing I was looking for a time-out avenue where I would be alone but not alone. I wanted to spend days and nights with no responsibilities, no phone calls, and no internet connection looking for me.

How does someone plan for a step-away trip created for one person? Without guilt and obligation and worry? I was about to find out as I was determined to take a few weeks away. A friend of mine continually takes a few weeks away every year and encouraged me to get in line and get it scheduled. She is successful in her business and family life and full of ideas and fun. So, I thought if she can do it……

I looked at Europe and Asia and Africa since I wanted this to be a solo adventure and far enough away that I felt the isolation of distance. The hotels had to be clean and updated, no doors facing the parking lot, English spoken as a first language since it's the only language I understand, and the city safe to walk and ride public transportation.

I set my sights on Melbourne, Australia but had second thoughts before boarding the flight which is when I asked myself what have I done. Too late to change and am now committed. I rolled my carry-on onto the plane, found my seat, and buckled in.

The silence felt like a living being that attached itself to me as I flew, walked, rode, slept, and ate. The silence of me all by myself in a crowd of strangers knowing no one, and being alone while not. The silence while I read, visited museums, listened to other conversations, tasted espresso, and sat by the water to watch the anemones. The silence called to me in a way I had never experienced.

It was loud and kind and thoughtful. It re-made me. I felt free and time stood still for 3 weeks. I lived in the silence of invisibility while I roamed the city and countryside.

Melbourne, the city of my silence, and writing, and nature, and architect, and color, and curious people willing to give direction and instruction to transit stops, I miss it today.

My friend is a happy person and there was not a little gloating over the fact that I spent 3 glorious weeks in Melbourne. Now she feels justified in her belief that I work too much. Really, maybe, possibly, and probably.

WHEN WORDS ARE SUPERIOR

Yesterday I spoke with a guy who was talking about selling his product in several facilities. He said that he meets with the front desk attendant or secretary for product purchase decisions or, if he is lucky, "someone of importance" his words, not mine.

And what followed was a few more disrespectful adjectives.

I was speechless! It took a few moments to catch myself and continue with the phone call.

My story is not about political correctness. Today I am not writing a word about p.c. No, this is about a belief that is so deep, so entrenched that the person spewing this crap is not even aware of what is wrong with his values. What is wrong with him?

Words can be superior. And in this case, I had the opportunity to respond.

I spoke no negative, hateful, critical words but the language of strength, encouragement, value determining, and respect.

Below are a few words I responded with to explain what I am emphasizing here.

Individual, friend, person, decision-maker, authority, partner, relationship.

All words that support human value without a "can you honestly believe position determines value" confrontation.

Words are superior, specifically when used to support, encourage, promote, and clarify value.

I never plan to disagree when attending an event or appointment, although sometimes I do, and then, I work at explaining, describing, and uplifting without confrontation.

My all-time favorite soapbox message is about treating employees and colleagues with respect, encouragement, and kindness. ....

This guy got the message loud and clear. And it showed because his tone and word usage changed the next minute. How terrifically wonderful if this short conversation started him on the awareness of "hey, everyone deserves respect" path.

I may not be able to change the world or my neighbor, but I am responsible for myself and the words that flow from my mouth. And this gives me hope that one word, one thoughtful word, might cause another person to stop, think and raise the bar on respect, love, life, and community.

Words are superior when used excellently!

WHEN WORRY IS UNDERVALUED

We often hear the phrase "don't worry about it"!

Or "what's to worry about?" or "it is a worrisome situation."

As often as I try not to worry about something, I fail.

I decided to change the story about worry. Since worry seems to be inevitable, why not embrace the good?

Last week I was a student at a training session in Buffalo, NY. I absorbed tremendous information through demonstrations and lectures on a new business. However, I worried through most of the three days about how this new business would affect current accounts and staffing.

Then I worried about understanding all the material and being able to transfer what I learned. Impossible, it seemed to me. So, then I worried about this being impossible.

Amy and Dave presented data, mockups, worst case, and shortcuts to starting. Amanda and Bethany covered table conversations, and Paul and Miles took on the technical details during our interactive sessions. It was a brain-full time.

And I kept worry by my side 24/7. What, when, how, and where?

And then worry worked for me.

All this time sitting with worry, going through scenarios to try this and that, approach this way or not, hire this person or work with current staff, the solution became clear.

Worry kept me in the game of moving the pieces and creating a new outcome.

Undervalued, overlooked, and highly effective.

WHERE ARE THE MANAGERS

We clean big buildings when there are hundreds of people working there. We have seen buildings during the good the bad and now the virus. We sit at the table with managers who want only the best for their buildings. These managers speak up and ask hard questions and expect good answers that are followed up with good results.

At the table the chairs are high-backed and comfortable, a wooden table brown or black, and most managers like eye-to-eye contact with a lot of what do you know attitude that keeps us all on our toes.

Then came the virus. Which brought us back at the table or as we saw in our business, learning the new meeting language of ZOOM. Okay now there appeared to be a major change in the how of moving information. In our industry the focus of cleaning from the position of safety, appearance, health, air quality expanded to getting rid of unwanted germs, viruses, bacteria by cleaning and disinfecting.

It became a new experience as we began to talk with each other in the cleaning world within the navigation of ZOOM.

I met some pretty terrific people on ZOOM. Their generosity showed in their posture especially when they leaned in on a laptop camera to be better understood and by following up to be sure there was clarity, always willing to reZOOM and talk once more to keep the project moving forward.

It seems today confusion and chaos rule the day with an overload of information everywhere, this is no exception in commercial cleaning.

Infection cleaning which goes by "disinfecting service" is unfamiliar to many managers and many vendors are knocking at the email door with high-flying images and colorful words that do not say anything of value.

As one concerned manager said, what is what with all of this?

Many of us process information best in the calm after the storm. Every manager has some idea of the best way to tackle their building during the transition and I believe that is where we are today. We are in a transition phase that calls for a few good people to make informed decisions to keep their building healthy.

I am confident that the outcome looks better from the other side. Remember the GOP convention a few years back, Tampa property managers nailed it in their planning and execution, it showed success all the way around.

Whether we have a ZOOM less life once everyone returns to their office or find a new way of meeting, like seeing each other in person, we can be certain we will see one another by a method that satisfies.

WHO IS THIS FOR? THE BUSINESS OF BUSINESS

At the networking event, a woman crying in the restroom was afraid to share her vulnerable self, believing that her authority at her office would be undermined if she did so.

At the luncheon event, the woman was afraid to go home, with no money, no support, and without the courage to change her miserable living arrangement.

The woman in the legal office, no longer driving to and from work or anywhere else for that matter, after a few no-fault accidents the past year, unable to rid herself of the fear she associates with being in the driver's seat.

I have often heard the stories of scared and feeling alone.

Until one day, I decided to tell my stories to chase away the scared and support and empathize with these women. I get it. I do.

I write to understand, explain, empathize, support, and educate people who find themselves wearing a face that isn't the one they live behind.

Sounds simple as this is every one of us at some time at someplace. I believe it doesn't need to be this way, or if it is, we can change it.

Not everyone, myself included, truly understands another person their situation.

Once I decided to tell the truth and show my humanness, I found out that that is the secret sauce to what is needed to make a connection.

I was speaking at an event where the crowd was in attendance to spend their money on a few heavy-duty investments. So, what did I talk about? The story of how I began my investing career. I described the silence in the car when I explained the investment plan to my husband and his no-reaction. I told the truth about driving through a downtrodden crime-ridden neighborhood and still not a single comment from my husband. Then I told the truth about my mention of "I might need to purchase a pickup with a guard dog in the passenger seat to do these kinds of investments," still no husband reaction. Finally, as we drove away from this part of the city, my husband turned to me and stated that maybe you better go and gain 100 pounds before you begin this investment strategy.

The audience went crazy and brought the house down.

This is for those who crave truth and acceptance in their humanness.

I did not always show up so that people saw my truth, but then I learned.

WHEN HOURS AWAY BECOME SACRED

I spent last week on a solo trip to Iceland.

Iceland has been a dream visit for me since time began, so when on Mother's Day my son, Peter, mentioned flights now flying into Reykjavik, I jumped on to the Delta site and booked my flight and hotel. Yes, this is what I did, and so glad I did.

As the travel date came nearer, I hesitated about the best way to see the sights and experience the island. I wanted to see Reykjavik and the landscape the island is famous for but hesitated about a tour bus ride. So, what to do? First, I checked to travel by taxi, way too expensive. Uber, nope, not happening in Iceland yet. Many local city and regional buses are possible but can be late, early, or not showing up, which I found too iffy.

My daughter, Janie, encouraged me countless times to rent a car, easy she said and entirely worth it. I was freaked out though, I had visions of encountering sheep-filled roads, lava pouring out on the asphalt, winds taking over, and pushing my car into oncoming traffic, no shoulders to elevate the fear of what happens if I need to pull over? And when I read about the narrow mountain pass roads at the high elevations, I thought of driving off into the abyss.

Back and forth, I analyzed and debated the best ways to take in and experience Iceland, and finally, I decided I would walk in the city and rent a car to drive the rural roads. It was the BEST decision ever!

The first few days, I walked the city. It was chilly, perfect temps for walking, and I found that people walk or ride these little two-wheel scooters on virtually every sidewalk. Totally easy. I got pretty good at dodging the scooters, exploring the coffee shops, and visiting the bookstores. Icelanders pride themselves on their authors, language skills, and literacy. Then, I discovered the city cemetery by accident. It is an expansive botanical garden without plant labels and paths. Instead, the greenery of trees and moss, and fungus covers the vast area. The stones are old and new, with names that genuinely leave a visitor with the sense of being in this foreign country. The paths are willy-nilly, so much so that it was easy to walk without finding a direct route from one side to the other and this way spend magical moments hearing the birds and feeling the peace.

After a few days in Reykjavik, I rented this little gray/blue car. It was missing a hubcap, had a few scratches, but it was the smallest vehicle Hertz had available. I was comforted that it came with navigation because the roads are narrow and windy and rough and sparse, and signs are in Icelandic. We are talking about titles and names 15 to 20 letters long. Fortunately, for me all navigation directions were in American English. Thankful. Oh, and I did not encounter a one-stop sign anywhere, but roundabouts and yields and traffic lights, that's it.

I found the sights from the country roads magnificent. So much to see and to absorb, which totally took me out of my ordinary. I think back to this time as a "clearing of my mind" because there was so much new and different and strange it boggles the expected and reframes my experience.

The lava fields flowed from old volcanic craters, the black covered with green and yellow moss. It was amazing. And there were roadside white flowers so tiny and fragile looking, bent over from the force of the wind. And, I saw colossal ocean waves pounding with such force the bird cries from overhead could not be heard, then the single church steeple off in the distance, solitary as a sentinel.

If I could only bring you there with me, open my head and put your brain alongside mine. So much life, feeling, power, and energy in the raw elements of the Icelandic landscape. Unbelievable and majestic while at the same time touchable and absorbable. Other-worldly, so much so that I found myself at times stopping just to listen and look.

Now a few basic driving related features. The rural main roads are accessible and sparsely traveled since almost all of the population of Iceland lives in the city. The secondary roads are rocky, gravelly, and pot-holey, but worth every jarring and prayer said in the hope of reaching my destination safely.

I ultimately think I was reborn on this short week in Iceland and I think I had the webs cleared out of my mind. And, for sure, I experienced the energy and essence of time alone, sitting, breathing, noticing, and being.

No big decisions were made, but plenty of appreciation of the unimaginable beauty seen.

Today, I revisit the overwhelming feeling of reverence and admiration of Iceland and my heart of full.

WHY 3 BOOKS

By my chair there is a small wooden table and next to this small table is a stack of books. These are books I am currently reading and have page markers or turned-over corners to keep my spot. I almost always have 3 books going at the same time.

Three different authors, very unlike one another with completely different ways of expressing their stories and ideas.

Why you might ask? It's just that there is so much to learn and reading different authors in different genres causes me to think differently, sometimes extraordinary thoughts show up in my head and I then I enjoy the challenge of these new ideas.

Growing up we didn't have many books in our home. The small elementary school I attended had 2 shelves of dusty smelly books, didn't matter how dusty and smelly though, I read every one and several more than once. The stories were magic as they shot me out of my daily life into a world that I longed to see and learn about.

But once I grew up and got married and then had kids and tons of responsibilities, reading for pleasure was put on the back burner but only for a short time. Since reading had been my hobby, my joy, my education, and my peace, I gravitated back to it for myself.

And then did what any mother would do, I taught my kids to read, to sit for hours in libraries and look at books, settling on the floor reading and page-turning. We spent afternoons at the library and evenings reading aloud a favorite author, a book series, that allowed us to visit a world that was sometimes familiar but most times strange and unknown.

I love books. I love what authors convey by their writing. I love sharing my love of books and authors with my children and now my grandchildren.

When I think of 3 books, I see 3 totally different authors creating their masterpiece of ideas and beliefs and bravely putting themselves out there by sharing their words with us, their readers, their supporters, and their encouragers.

With books, words on the page can become personal to the reader, magic.

WHY GOOD WORK?

Good work for ourselves sake.

When the work is done at night or where no one sees, why good work?

This is the question of the day or night when your business activity is primarily working evening and night hours.

Cleaning carpet when no one is about or cares. Pressure washing the entry and sidewalk during the night, having more fun with the power sprayer than getting the last gum split removed.

Why good work?

We talk about work quality at our company meetings, as we sit around the board room table and translate from Spanish to English.

My personal belief is that work, outstanding work, and doing the best I can, leave me happier with myself. Can I get better? Sure, probably, most likely, but for right now, this is the best for me.

This personal belief is not shared by everyone. But, I mean, what's wrong with doing what it takes to get by, fewer steps, maybe.

In a word: Commitment. To oneself most of all.

Last week an electrician did some work in my home. A few simple light dimmers in the dining and kitchen. I was okay with a minor glitch. He was not. As he said, "no, this has to be perfect," he continued to make it perfect.

He is an excellent example of commitment to oneself, which is why his workmanship is in high demand.

Is our commitment to good work front and center? Who cares?

We, us, you and me.

Why the Shuffle

Last Tuesday, I walked into the office with a skip in my step and ready to take on ANYTHING!

That was until I heard a few people already in the office on a terror about government, kids, and other drivers. Then, petty and unkind comments slowed my step and put a hitch in my breath.

I found that my skip of ready for anything took a shuffle. Just like that, I was deflated and unhappy.

I do not know what was different about that day than any other, but I do know for some crazy reason, I stopped and took note of what was going on around me. I zeroed in on how I felt before, during, and after hearing the grumblings and complaints.

And then I took a long look at myself and asked the pertinent question, when am I like this with other people? When do I complain, whine, and basically make others miserable? When do I act out without any thought of others, and how it affects them?

That Tuesday night, I sat outside under the tree canopy on my deck and decided to wake up and pay attention to my actions and words and how they affect the people around me, in this case, my office staff. Have I done this internal look-see before? Yes, and now it was time for me to revisit it yet again.

What frustrates me about myself is my lack of remembering. In this case, I had an internal check when I heard and saw others in the office acting out. Now, if only I would not need the reminder.

Maybe, someday this will be automatic. Maybe, someday.

WHY THE SHUFFLE

Last Tuesday, I walked into the office with a skip in my step and ready to take on ANYTHING!

That was until I heard a few people already in the office on a terror about government, kids, and other drivers. Then, petty and unkind comments slowed my step and put a hitch in my breath.

I found that my skip of ready for anything took a shuffle. Just like that, I was deflated and unhappy.

I do not know what was different about that day than any other, but I do know for some crazy reason, I stopped and took note of what was going on around me. I zeroed in on how I felt before, during, and after hearing the grumblings and complaints.

And then I took a long look at myself and asked the pertinent question, when am I like this with other people? When do I complain, whine, and basically make others miserable? When do I act out without any thought of others, and how it affects them?

That Tuesday night, I sat outside under the tree canopy on my deck and decided to wake up and pay attention to my actions and words and how they affect the people around me, in this case, my office staff. Have I done this internal looksee before? Yes, and now it was time for me to revisit it yet again.

What frustrates me about myself is my lack of remembering. In this case, I had an internal check when I heard and saw others in the office acting out. Now, if only I would not need the reminder.

Maybe, someday this will be automatic. Maybe, someday.

WOMEN + 3

Three women who shaped the person I am today

I read a true story about a single woman who rode her horse from Maine to California in the 1950s. One woman, 2 horses, and a dog traversed roads unknown to see the Pacific Ocean. It is an unforgettable story that steered me in wanting to learn more about the women in my life who came before me.

The first complication I discovered is that women do not talk about themselves all that much, at least not in my lineage. I probed my mother with questions about her early life, marriage, and daily thoughts. Her one continued response was: we don't talk about that, or it's over, and there is no need to bring it up. WHAT! Ok, now it was time for me to go off-script and dig. I discovered more about these beautiful women through photos and writings, and I was not above prying questions.

My maternal grandmother, Bertha Loch Peitz, married, had a family, raised chickens, sold eggs, worked at grading tobacco leaves. In today's language, we would use these labels representing her adult life: A partner in Peitz Farm, a Poultry Vendor, and a Controller at Tobacco Plant.

Grandma Peitz was a woman with a significant presence, always dressed with a flowered apron; she loved playing cards. Steady, tenacious, and with a ready smile and willingness to enter into any conversation. My Mom earnestly reminds me that Grandma Peitz had a tough life; I am thankful she stuck with it and showed up and was the mother my mom admired.

My paternal grandmother was my step-grandmother; Ida Grotz Broll married my grandfather when his first wife passed, leaving him with two children. Ida brought a daughter into the marriage, and they had a daughter together. A real yours, mine and our family. The mystery of Ida's daughter remained just that a secret; this was one of the times where my mom told me, "We don't talk about it." I was close to my Grandma Ida Broll; we spent a lot of time together in her later years. She was a tiny woman, barely 4'4". Her business was Gardener and Garden Stand Vendor in that she planted, weeded, and managed a garden and sold pints of raspberries and bags of vegetables every summer. This woman had a brutal introduction to adulthood, unmarried with a daughter, then married and inherited two stepchildren (who were profoundly mourning their mother's passing) and then giving birth to another child. Managing all of that, kids, housework, gardening, vendors, it had to be tough. One thought to remember is that this was in the 1920s. The Code of Silence for women was alive and active in our country.

And lastly, I want to highlight my mom in just a few sentences. Dolores Peitz Broll married young, had 11 children, Partner, and Administrator in Broll Farm, Saleswoman, Poultry, Egg Vendor, Board Member, Non-Profit Organizer.

When Mom tells stories of her growing up years, she always comments on the weather and the work. I believe that is because she was raised on a farm and spent a large share of her adult life managing a farm. It's in her blood. Weather and Work.

There is so much I could say about my mom's life. But the thread that runs through my memories is steady and tenacious, keeping on by keeping on, just like her mom! I would also add encourager and cheerleader. No matter what crazy idea I come up with or business plan or travel destination, my mom is on board and seeing the benefit in the doing.

So, there you go, my two grandmothers and my mom were huge influences as I was growing up, and in a nutshell, I wrote about them here. There are certainly more questions that are calling for an answer.

Grandma Peitz, why did she choose employment in a tobacco plant? Grandma Broll, how did she speak up in her marriage? Mom, why couldn't we have pets in the house when we were little kids?

Gratitude fills me as I write the real stories of the women in my family who didn't give up, give in or give away their strength and loyalty to family. Today, I am thankful.

WORDS WITHOUT SOUND

My sister-in-law, Judy, is a straight-shooter, direct and clear about her opinions and what's what. Then one day not all that long ago, she found out that she was seriously sick, so much so, the family gathered and sat with her during a warm, sunny, weekend.

There I sat, taking in the conversation, the laughter, and love of everyone around the patio table, noticing that Judy did not add her two cents, this was unusual, then I realized it was more what she did not say, even more, when she gave me a look. I began to pay close attention.

When Judy looked at me out of her big b chair at the patio table with the sun shining and the baby robins bobbing their little heads in their nest high above.

They sat Judy at the head of the table, with those big blue eyes and speaking the language of spirit to spirit.

And before I left, she glanced at me again, and I felt that she was speaking directly, a message that I was to understand. So, I listened when she rested her eyes on me, and this is what I heard.

My body is perfect, I am ready to leave it. I am happy, I am joyful, I am love, can you feel it? Can you see it? Can you touch it?

That unforgettable afternoon, Judy, in her no-nonsense way of delivery, gave me a gift and a message, the gift that we can die with dignity and the message that words are not necessary.

WORK AS A LANGUAGE

I automatically put up a deflective guard when asked what do you do? I stumble because honestly, how does a person describe all the variations, such as considering wage increases, buying business insurance, or traveling from Minneapolis to Tampa? And yet, it is what I do.

I see a correlation with life today, and the years my kids were young, and I was forehead stamped with the label, "stay at home mom." During those years, I was often changing diapers and, at the same time, working out when I could get back to the ledgers to enter numbers in the bookkeeping journals I kept.

But it wasn't until I read an aguage idea into practice. When the woman beside me asked what I do on my last flight, I chatted about the guys who work with me, one in particular, and his determination years ago in coming to the US from Cuba and doing so on a raft. She got it, and she understood my job by this short 60-second story.

No preparation or memorization is required—just an actual life event, short and sweet.

I find myself wanting to do this more often. It might be the best way the language of my work expands.

And not a tagline.

We are not titles, though, at times, titles are necessary. Instead, we might be the language of work.

WORKING IN A FOREIGN STATE

I have always loved the stories about business ownership and growth and management and because of the interest, I read a ton of books and attended many seminars and classes that supported my business/ownership story-fix.

And then I got the opportunity of a lifetime.

When a business came for sale in Florida in the industry, I was familiar with I jumped at the chance to be the owner with the agreement of my family that I would travel back and forth from Minnesota to manage and grow the Florida business.

Soon after the purchase contract was signed, I rearranged the business as I felt was necessary and now, I was searching the market for more employees and new accounts. This is where I hit a huge snag. My experience in previous ownership was centered in the Midwest and I foolishly thought that what a person wanted in Minnesota would also want in Florida. NOT SO.

Commissions, payroll frequency, uniforms, identification, background checks, and licensing to name just a few differences. My expectation was the biggest change for me. There were days I felt like I was doing business in another country, the differences were so markedly different.

Not only were staffing differences noticeable, but the air also smelled warm, the trees had moss art hanging from the limbs, the flowers seemed the brightest of reds, the streets had names I could not pronounce, the houses were cement and tile-roofed ALL UNLIKE anywhere I had lived before. In those early days, I often felt like I was in a foreign state.

Then I began to notice the small shops on one of the main thoroughfares and marveled at the different names and foods and products offered. I asked about these shops and who the owners were and where they originated from. Were they a family business or a large corporation? Mostly, these small footprints of space were family-owned businesses.

I was sold.

How could I have predicted this newness of my life of people and ways of doing business? I do not think it would have been possible if I had not experienced a first-hand look and felt the energy of one small business after another small business all lined up tight on the street, every business offering a product or service.

I have changed. The characteristics I understood of small business were quite limited pre- Florida. Currently, I am at the mid-Florida mark and I now better understand employees, culture, language, products, and the owners that have their own unique way. Embracing and accepting and learning while keeping to my strict standards, only making the change of incorporating new with the already proven.

Forever Grateful.

WORKING WITH HONORABLE PEOPLE

This week I was stuck in making my own problem. Out of my utter unawareness, a couple of the technicians were out of certification compliance. In my industry, this is a big deal. Ugh. The worst, though, was that we needed these two techs in keeping with a visual show of certification within the next couple of weeks.

The out-of-compliance became known when we prepared for printing the certificate for each technician for the upcoming RFP. Unpleasant surprise!

Year after year, we train and make sure every technician, manager, and I are certified in the cleaning we offer to our customers. And now this, right when we are amid spreadsheets and calculations and paperwork.

The worst part was that I thought all I would need to do was email the certifying agency and resolve this immediately. I was wrong.

We are talking here about time zone differences, more than one person to reach out to, and me doing the reaching out. I stumbled through the call and emails and came up with nothing. No solution, and our immediate problem was unresolved.

We were now under the wire for time and delivery, and deadline. So, I contacted the agency several times and was piecemealing a solution, but it was not coming together, and then I thought about a guy I knew who worked closely with this agency.

Because I have not asked for permission from this person to print his name, let's just call him Paul.

One email and phone call to Paul changed everything. He took on the responsibility of working with the agency to get the certs needed to submit the RFP. Paul worked his magic and kept at it until he reached the solution and figured out the certs' confusion.

I am so happy that the current 2021-2022 certificates will be here in time, and our RFP will be complete within the submission timeline.

Paul did not have to stick out his neck for us. This was totally his decision. He has no skin in the game here. But Paul is an honorable guy who relishes the joy of helping others when he can.

And us? We thank Paul and the stars for the relationship we have with an honorable person.

WORKING HERE THEN THERE

Becoming a business owner sort of snuck up on me. For years I worked with my husband in managing service businesses in Minnesota. It was fulfilling and I was flexible with our family commitments and home office hours. This worked all the way around for our family and for me.

Then our youngest daughter graduated from high school and left for Army boot camp, I knew I had to make a change for myself and so I began looking for a business I could buy and build for myself, just me as the owner. I wanted to be responsible for all major decisions and on-the-block if something went wrong. I wanted to hire, manage, organize and strategize.

But there were limitations on the type of business I was familiar with and ready to step into. Working alongside my husband taught me a lot about business management, I picked up a few professional executive certificates and attended a couple business management boot camps over the years, and now I was quite sure I was ready to be the business owner I envisioned.

I looked for just the right business, near to where we lived and, in the industry, I was comfortable in. Couldn't find a fit until I spread the net wider and discovered a desirable business for sale in Tampa. I hadn't ever been to Tampa, but this was sure worth the flight.

Long story short, I flew down in November and closed on the business in December, What a terrific decision. 17 years later and my commute to and from Tampa-Minneapolis has fit wonderfully into my lifestyle and the business is totally satisfying for me as the owner. I have learned so much that is not written or taught in a class or forum or book.

Were there and are there still challenges, you bet. Professional and personal growth, absolutely. I wouldn't change it all for the world.

I have seen that life happens while we are looking for life, strange, isn't it? Buying this business 17 years ago and being in the moment was the only way I could run, manage and make the decisions I have made to keep it going successfully for myself and my staff. What a good decision all those years ago.

No regrets.

YOU HAVE GOT TO READ THIS

Every few days, I read why staffing is a significant headache for zillions of businesses. Unfortunately, the reasons are valid and severe.

Too late, too slow, too unworkable, too independent, too money-wanting, too unrealistic, too many false expectations and the list expands,

If I had the magic formula, I believe I would be on prime-time news every day in every city.

The truth is that I do not have a magic formula, but I do have a proven track record of keeping employees.

Last night we had an employee event. From the laughing, yelling, and air-punching, I took that to mean it was successful, which got me thinking about staff hiring, keeping, and productivity.

I am writing this short page to give the reader, you, my two cents worth of experience hiring and keeping staff. Hoping you will get something you can work on within your business.

MOST IMPORTANT: love your employees. Yes, I love them! Do you ask about their interests or consider the small talk a waste of time. Are you too busy to connect by looking everyone in the eye when they are near?

Hire friends of good employees. And sometimes, this is family. I shuttered to do this the first time. But now I find that friends and family are good hires. They have similar attributes and work ethics. Hiring from within changed my business from lackadaisical to efficient and trustworthy.

Have small events that employees like, not what you want. I have a whole different set of likes, and when I tried a few, they bombed. So, ok, lesson learned. Before I or my GM schedules a staff event/fun time, we stop and check to be sure this is all about them and not for our benefit. And this goes for the food, activity, and time of day.

Back to last night. I was thrilled by the reception of the raffle, where everyone wins. I know that happiness breeds goodwill, and for sure, our building held much pleasure yesterday.

These events are all about the staff, but sometimes I feel like a mouse in the corner, not seen but receiving a gigantic basket of benefits.

Let's summarize what works. Love your staff. Plan activities they enjoy. Hire from within whenever it makes sense.

Then you can expect people to show up once the word gets out that you are the person to work with, and I am talking about working with and not working for; please understand that your terminology matters

ABOUT THE AUTHOR

Marleen Geyen is a dedicated business owner and community member living in Minnesota with her husband. She is surrounded by a lively family, including four adult children, their spouses, and nine grandchildren. Marleen's passion for business and family life enriches her insights, which she shares in her writings. She can be reached for advice and collaboration at M Business Advisors (marleengeyen@gmail.com)

www.ingramcontent.com/pod-product-compliance
Lightning Source LLC
Chambersburg PA
CBHW061023220326
41597CB00019BB/3152

* 9 7 9 8 8 9 3 2 4 4 7 8 6 *